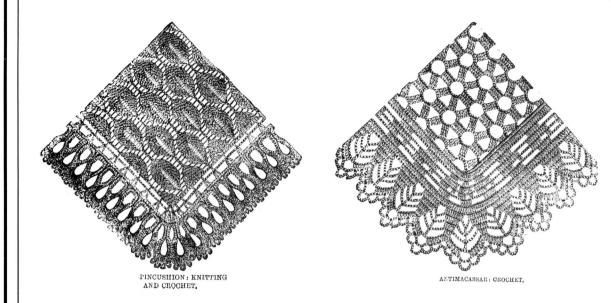

PINCUSHION: KNITTING
AND CROCHET.

ANTIMACASSAR: CROCHET.

KNITTED COUNTERPANE.

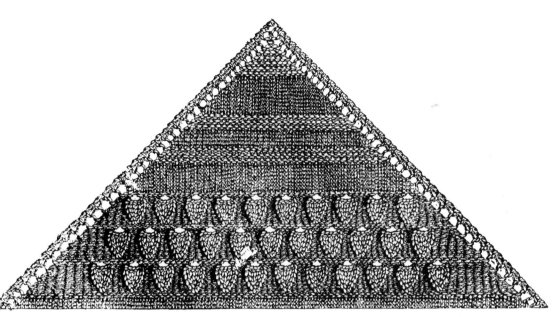

HALF OF KNITTED SQUARE FOR COUNTERPANE.

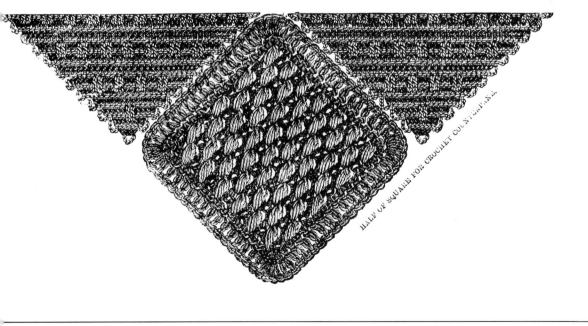

HALF OF SQUARE FOR CROCHET COUNTERPANE.

Traditional Victorian White Work

to Knit and Crochet for the Home

Shelagh Hollingworth

St. Martin's Press ● New York

Photographs by Brian Hollingworth

Line drawings by Giles Hollingworth

Library of Congress Cataloging-in-Publication Data

Hollingworth, Shelagh.
   Traditional Victorian white work to knit and crochet for the
home.

   1. Knitting—Patterns.   2. Crocheting—Patterns.
3. Decorative arts, Victorian.   I. Title.
TT820.H776   1987   746.9   87–12994
   ISBN 0–312–01552–6
   ISBN 0–312–01253–5 (pbk)

First published in Great Britain by B. T. Batsford Ltd., under the
title *Knitting and Crochet for the Home*.

Typeset by Latimer Trend & Company Ltd, Plymouth
and printed in Great Britain by R. J. Acford Ltd, Chichester

First U.S. Edition

10 9 8 7 6 5 4 3 2 1

Contents

Introduction

The origins of knitting and crochet are acknowledged to be obscure and are wide open to speculation. For the purposes of this book we need look back no further than the Victorian era, that period of extremes of fortune in Great Britain, when the wealthy were worlds apart from the poor. Most of that social history is well documented elsewhere.

In those days the rich had very high moral standards and the time to indulge them. The ladies responded to this attitude simply by covering anything and everything with embellishment, from handkerchiefs to piano legs. On the other hand the poor, if they were in employment at all, worked such long hours that they had no spare time for handicrafts and were fortunate indeed to have even the basics of furniture, let alone fancy pieces with legs that needed covering from view.

Working-class mothers were housebound and accepted that this was their place in life. Knitting and crochet were a form of pastime that was approved for any moments of rest. They would possibly knit for the children, make gloves, socks, scarves, shawls and hats for all the family, and a variety of undergarments now long out of fashion. This would keep them busy enough, but they might also find time to work linen edgings or a bedspread for a daughter's dowry, although this would be something special, and dowry items belonged more to the upper classes.

Another group of ladies was drawn from what would now be termed the middle class – those whose wealth was too recently acquired for them to be accepted as gentry. These ladies had time on their hands but could not appear to be making items for themselves. The accepted way to make use of their spare time was to form or join knitting or sewing circles. They would meet in each others' houses, take tea and probably gossip too while they worked at their handicraft, which generally provided articles for the benefit of the poorer classes. This was indeed a strange state of affairs; the working class was literally slaving away to provide reasonably priced, ready-made items for the upper class who in turn used its spare time to produce handmade items for the poor.

Two things altered this way of life. The World Wars of this century caused attitudes to the working class to alter, primarily because women's roles in the factories changed: they had become an important labour source. The trade union movement was another prime mover in the way that factories and shops were run. People began to be better paid and this, with the influx of cheaper goods from abroad, made for better living conditions, and the necessity for handicrafts began to decline. To make things by hand could be taken by some to mean that one lacked the cash to buy ready-made. So handwork had a social stigma and knitting was confined to garments made for children. Fortunately there had been a rise in educational values and many more people were able to read and write. With this skill came the advent of printed patterns, so that although articles may not have been made in such profusion, the methods and instructions were recorded for posterity.

Knitting in particular has remained a popular pastime and in the 1960s crochet enjoyed a revival in the fashion world, but no one could have foreseen the recent, unprecedented rise in the popularity of handknit fashion wear. This is partly due to the beautiful yarns presently being manufactured and to changing attitudes to the craft. Simple and practical knitwear is still cheap enough to be purchased ready-made and with all the leisure time we have we can now knit or crochet for the pleasure it gives us.

'Back to romanticism' seems to be the keynote, and if we can take up our yarn and knitting needles or crochet hooks and make something beautiful, we can not only complement our homes with a touch of our own personality but possibly also provide an heirloom for tomorrow.

Equipment and working methods

Many of the patterns provided here are for traditional articles brought up to date. We can also take advantage of modern methods and yarns, etc. to accomplish the finest possible handwork. Reference is made to the equipment that might have been used for the original items and to suitable materials available today. It is not necessary to restrict oneself to the suggested materials – trying out different yarns with the patterns will possibly result in an entirely new and novel piece of work.

Equipment

Yarns

Most articles for the home would have been made originally in pure cotton yarns. These were cheap, readily available and pleasant to work with. They would not have the brilliant white look that today is obtained by modern technology, but white was tremendously popular in Victorian times. Indeed, this period has been described as the one of 'Victorian white knitting', referring to the articles that come under that heading, for example bedspreads (the smaller lap-rugs were also known as *couvre-pieds*), antimacassars, table linen, etc. Later, during the 1920s, experiments in the textile trades produced manmade yarns such as artificial silk (probably a term for rayon and similar threads), but these lacked one great advantage that pure cotton had: cotton could be bleached. Articles in the home needed constant washing and bleaching would have been part of that task.

   In keeping, therefore, with that tradition, most of the items in this book are worked in cotton yarns. This is still the best textile to use to produce a completed article as near to the original as possible. Cotton is strong, it washes well and it will last for generations. Softer yarns might be more suitable for the baby covers, but try making these in light cotton yarns to make comfortable covers for spring or summer babies.

Knitting needles and crochet hooks

There are plenty of examples of Victorian handwork tools to be seen in museums. Not much has altered about these over the years except the materials used in their manufacture. Victorian needles and hooks were either of bone or ivory and, no doubt, occasionally they could be fashioned in wood. Between the Wars certain plastics were introduced and knitting needles became much lighter to work with. This was only partly an advantage, as the weight of the knitting was inclined to bend the needles. This made them difficult to work with and could spoil the quality of the knitting.

The Second World War produced some strange, new manmade substances, probably the most important being nylon. Nylon was thought to be the answer to everything and was used wherever possible. Not only was it spun into yarn but it could be used to form rigid items such as needles, hairbrushes, etc. These were soon displaced by the advent of other plastics with long, unpronounceable names that provided us with plastic-covered steel needles which remained rigid for the finer sizes, and solid plastic for the thicker sizes which also remained rigid. Crochet hooks were made in the same materials and a certain uniformity was arrived at. Gauges became widely available and not only were the knitting needles uniform in style, but they were also manufactured to strict size gradings that could be tested by the knitter.

Nowadays, as if to underline the saying that there is nothing new under the sun, the latest innovations in knitting needles are a return to natural materials. It is now possible to purchase knitting needles made of bamboo, wood and substances similar to whalebone. All knitting needles and crochet hooks need to be replaced periodically, especially when working in white yarns – the tips of the needles wear thin and the metal may cause the knitting to turn grey – and now might be a good time to invest in some of the latest natural-feel needles. Certainly these are the most comfortable to use with natural fibres.

Tension and measurements

This is usually the part that knitters dread most because it impresses upon them the need to keep to the tension stated on the pattern and involves making lots of little squares, when all one wishes to do is start to make the actual article. To make the items described here, the tension is not vital, although if you wish the finished piece to measure exactly the measurements given in the pattern, it will be necessary to work to the tension stated. The most important reason for considering the tension is not so much the size of the stitches as the texture of the fabric obtained by using a particular pair of needles or hook with a particular type of yarn. If the square is hard and feels solid then try again using thicker needles or hook – you are probably working too tightly. If your sample square is too floppy and perhaps has holes where there shouldn't be holes, then the square has probably been worked too loosely and a finer pair of needles or hook should be tried.

Once you have a square that is neither too hard nor too floppy, then you are ready to begin. Remember that a whole bedspread is heavy, and if it is worked too tightly it will not hang loosely over the bed. Conversely, squares worked too loosely will produce a bedspread that grows in shape before your very eyes and trails all over the floor.

The tension given in the patterns here is a guide for that particular item and indicates the needles or hook that was used to make the article in the corresponding photograph. If you want to experiment with different yarns, needles or hooks, you will come up with different tensions and measurements. This is fine provided you keep to the rule that the fabric is neither so tight that the square is solid, nor so loose that it stretches readily.

Quantities

The quantities suggested for each item are those needed to provide a finished article worked to the tension given and with the completed measurements.

The best way to check whether you are going to have sufficient yarn is first to make sure that the tension is as near to perfect as possible with your initial square, then to carry on and see how many squares you can make from one ball. The pattern will tell you how many squares are required, so simply divide the total number of required squares by the number from one ball and the result is the number of balls required for the whole article.

It is very easy to calculate the total amount you will need if you are going to design an article for yourself, as long as you build on the separate-sections principle. First, experiment with yarns and needle or hook size. Once you have produced the square you really like, draw up a chart to show exactly how you will want the pieces arranged for finishing. This is best drawn on a sheet of squared paper (see Fig. 1). Measure your original square and mark that measurement out on the paper. At this stage you will be able to add or subtract a few squares to make the finished piece as large or as small as you require it, but do remember to allow a little for seams and for borders. Now that your working chart is completed you will be able to calculate the total number of pieces, and, as described in the tension and measurements section, you will have a true guide to check the required quantities. Divide the total number of squares needed by the number of squares that can be made from one ball and you will have the number of balls required. Do not restrict yourself to the exact number – always have a little in reserve if possible. Apart from needing yarn for edgings and borders, you will need yarn for making up the article and a big item, such as a bedspread, can easily take as much as a whole extra ball.

This rule for calculating yarn requirements carries over to the borders too, especially where they are quite wide. Work a whole ball in the border pattern and note the length that is obtained. Compare this measurement with the total length required and allow a suitable amount before beginning the work.

It could be argued that if white is used then there is not the urgent necessity to set aside the total amount of yarn, but even with white there can be slight variations between dye-lots, and white shows up any difference as clearly as colour.

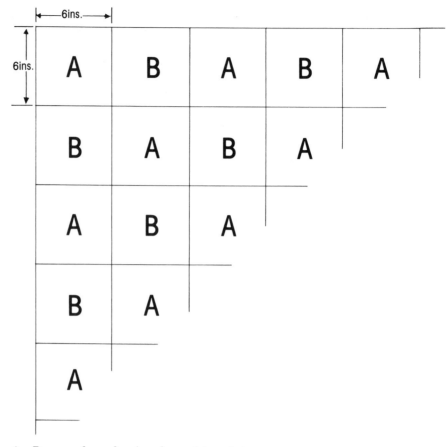

1 *Draw a chart showing the position of the squares*

Working methods

One of the advantages of the patterns in this book is that they are composed of small sections that are worked separately and joined together at the end of the handwork.

Since the items are meant to be worked at a leisurely pace, this piece-knitting or crochet is extremely convenient. It can be picked up and put down when there are only a few minutes to spare and it is a hobby that is easily transported. A little notebook is a useful accessory to keep a check on which row you stop at if you are suddenly called away, to note down the number of pieces as you make them and also to make sure that you are working the correct number of pieces.

Keep a close watch on the squares – it is all too easy to let some become rather loose through lack of concentration or possibly rather tight if you are working under pressure. This may not seem important but it will make the squares difficult to line up for sewing together.

Do not treat the pieces casually, for example by thrusting them down into the bottom of the knitting bag as they are finished. Keep them stored neatly and as flat as possible – this presents a much happier aspect when you come to the somewhat daunting task of making up.

As each square is finished, darn in all the loose ends. Facing the sewing together of, say, 48 or more squares is quite unnerving, but to be faced with all the ends as well could be enough to make you leave that beautiful handwork unfinished in a drawer for months. It is not a good idea to leave long ends for seaming – sew in all the ends, and if they are long enough to be used later for seaming, keep the trimmings separately for this purpose. The long ends never seem to be in the right place when it comes to making up. The correct method for joining seams is to join in new yarn as you need it, not where it happens to be at the end of making a square.

Making up

First, make certain that all the required pieces have been completed. It can be most disappointing to come to what is apparently the end of a huge piece of handwork only to find that there are some sections still to be made. Count the squares or strips, and if possible arrange them in the finished order. Simply counting the number may result in the correct number but not necessarily the order that you have visualised.

Traditional bedcovers in which the squares form an optical illusion are best sewn together with the right side of the work facing the worker (that is, with wrong sides together), using a mattress or invisible seam (see Fig. 2). This will make the join flat and virtually invisible so that, ideally, the viewer is unable to tell how the pattern has been contrived. Always join four sections into a larger square before continuing further; that is, join four small squares into a larger square until all the large squares are made, then join the large squares into lines. Finally join the lines of larger squares (see Fig. 3).

Where crochet squares are to be handsewn together these also are best joined into larger squares first. If the individual squares or strips have double crochet or trebles along the side edges these may be neatly joined with simple oversewn seams. Place the edges right sides together, work a neat oversewn seam along one side, working through the back loops of the stitches only. When turned to the right side of the work the seam is outlined by the front loops of the stitches. For joining squares, work two separate pairs of aligned squares along one edge and fasten off, then unfold the two sets of squares and place them, together, right sides facing, working

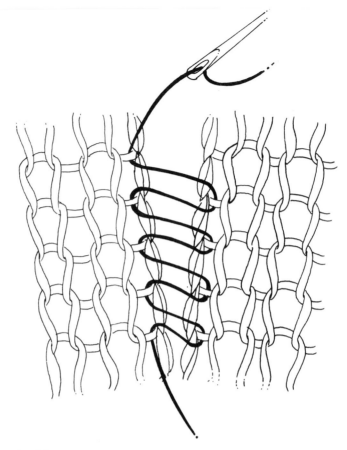

2   *Mattress seam*

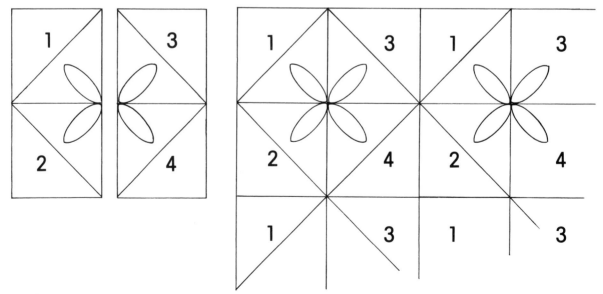

3   *Sequence for joining squares*

a seam along the adjacent sides to form a large square (see Fig. 4).

For a raised decorative effect, both knitted and crocheted sections can be joined with crochet seams. Hold two edges wrong sides together so that the edge stitches or rows may be matched exactly and, using a suitable crochet hook and matching yarn, insert the hook through both layers of fabric, draw loop through, yarn round hook and draw through loops on hook, forming a double crochet ridge on the right side of the work. It may not be appropriate to work into every stitch or row-end – adjust the double crochet to form as straight a line as possible. If the raised edge should flute or gather this will spoil the finished look.

Squares can also be joined with crochet slip stitch. Here, put the right sides of the work together and simply draw a loop through the work and through the loop on the hook before moving on to insert the hook into the next place. This method has the advantage of speed, since there is virtually no stopping to cut and re-thread the yarn as in hand sewing.

Joining the pieces into larger sections presents no difficulties but when the final seaming has to be done on a bedspread, for example, the work will be very heavy. It is best to work the last sections and the borders with the main part of the article supported upon a table.

If you have taken care to keep the individual sections relatively flat, the completed work should not require much finishing in the way of pressing, etc. Cotton yarn has a certain natural quality which ensures that the finished work stays relatively flat but does not lose its texture. Pressing should only be undertaken if it is absolutely necessary and attention must be given to the yarn label which will give full details about iron heat, etc.

Some items may be improved by 'dressing'. The article should be lightly rolled inside a dampened bathtowel and left for some hours to absorb the dampness. Then it should be carefully removed from the towel without being creased and left to dry out thoroughly in a completely flat position, ideally on an unused bed.

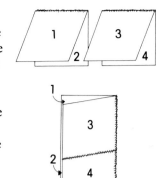

4   *Sewing order for crochet squares*

Making a start

Do not be afraid to embark on one of these projects. Remember that when you have made the first square or strip you are that much nearer to finishing. It can be very gratifying to mark off each square as you complete it.

If you would like to tackle a bedspread but feel a little daunted by the size of the task, begin by working, say, eight of the squares and joining them into a large cushion. This will provide you with a timetable from which to work and you will be able to gauge just how long a whole bedspread would take. You may carry on with the squares, and at the end you will have a matching cushion, or if you tire earlier you may unstitch

13

the cushion cover and use the pieces to complete the bedspread.

Some of the crochet articles are joined up as they are worked. If you embark on too large a project, many of these patterns will rest quite happily as a smaller item if you wish to stop. Small squares start out as a traycloth, then they can develop into a tablecloth, and if you cannot stop they could end as a bedspread, or a full-length window screen.

For those of you in a hurry or those who do not hand knit, knitting pattern 8 is for a bedspread, to be worked on a simple chunky knitting machine system. This serves merely as a starter – machine knitters can experiment by making squares on their own machines in the wide variety of yarns that are available to them and produce either traditional-style articles in a fraction of the handknit time, or, by virtue of their individual skill, invent a whole new series of original, unique items for the home.

Most of the projects suggested in this book lend themselves to being adapted to readers' ideas. The edgings, for example, can be used on bedlinen, but worked in other yarns or colours would look equally good as shelf-edgings against natural textures such as wood, and would serve to show off your china and glass.

These patterns show how household articles have been made traditionally. There is still room for originality. Try experimenting with the patterns, using other yarns. A whole new range of exciting fabrics will appear and you will be adding a touch of your own personality to a never-ending tradition.

Basic steps in knitting and crochet

It is often assumed that knitting and crochet are crafts learned in childhood and never forgotten. However, for many these skills can be allowed to disappear completely and may only be nudged into life at the sight of some article so attractive that the viewer cannot wait to make one exactly like it.

For such readers the following elementary instructions are given, briefly covering casting on stitches, basic knit and purl, casting off, basic chain crochet, double crochet and treble. Instructions are also given for increasing and decreasing in knitting. In crochet the decreases and increases are generally given in the text since they form part of the pattern instructions.

Knitting stitches and methods

Casting on

A neat and supple cast-on edge is achieved by the two-needle method. This is worked between the stitches and is sometimes called rope edge. On no account should the following row be worked into the back of the cast-on stitches as this simply tightens the edge.

Make a slip knot and place the loop on the left-hand needle. With this needle held in the left hand, take the second needle in the right hand and insert the point of the right-hand needle into the loop from left to right. Using the right hand, take the main yarn (from the ball) under the point of the right-hand needle, round between the needles, then holding the main yarn slightly taut, draw the main yarn loop through the slip knot to form a new loop on the right-hand needle. Using the left-hand needle point transfer this new loop on to the left needle.

To make the next stitch, insert the right needle point *between* the two stitches on the left needle, wrap the main yarn round the needle point and between the needles and draw through a new loop, then transfer this loop on to the left needle as before. Repeat this movement until all the stitches are cast on.

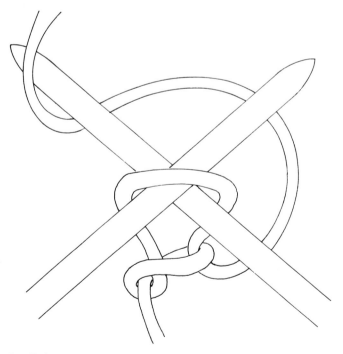

5 *Take yarn under point of needle*

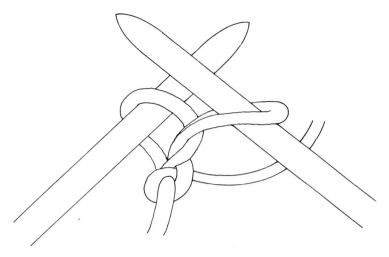

Knit stitch

Having cast on the required number of stitches, it is probably necessary to knit a tension sample and you will need to be able to work both basic knitting and purl for this purpose.

Hold the needle with the cast-on stitches in the left hand and the empty needle in the right hand. Insert the point of the right-hand needle into the first stitch on the left needle from left to right, with the main yarn at the back of the work. Now, taking the yarn in the right hand, wrap it under the point of the right needle and round between the two needle points and slightly back. With the right needle draw back the point to bring through the main yarn loop, forming a new stitch on the right-hand needle, and let the old stitch slip off the left needle point. One stitch has now been knitted. Continue in this way, knitting across the row. At the end of the row, turn the work to place the needle with the stitches in the left hand and the empty needle in the right hand.

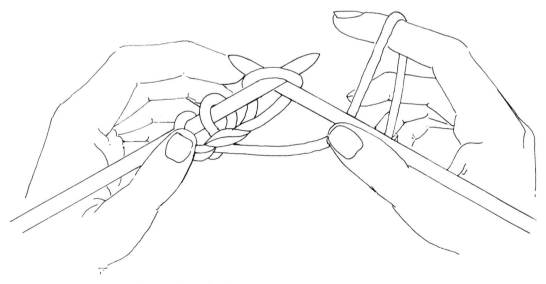

7 *Insert point of right needle into first stitch*

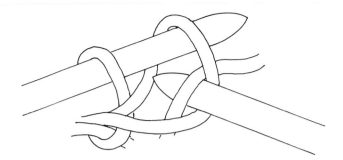

8 *Draw back the point of right needle*

Garter stitch is worked in this way, knitting every row. It may be made neater if the first stitch of every row is slipped knitwise (as if to knit). Where garter stitch ridges are needed in patterns it is sometimes more convenient to begin the pattern on the wrong side of the work, in which case purl rows may be specified – this will produce exactly the same effect since knit and purl simply make stitches towards either the front of the work or the back.

Purl stitch

Take the needle holding the cast-on stitches in the left hand. With the empty needle in the right hand, insert the point of the right needle into the first stitch on the left needle, from right to left, with the main yarn to the front of the work. Holding the main yarn in the right hand, take the main yarn round the point of the right needle, first between the two needle points then under the right needle, and draw the yarn back. Turning the needle right and away, draw the main yarn loop through the left loop and on to the right needle. Let the stitch slip off the left-hand needle. One stitch has been purled on to the right-hand needle. Continue in this way until all the stitches have been worked.

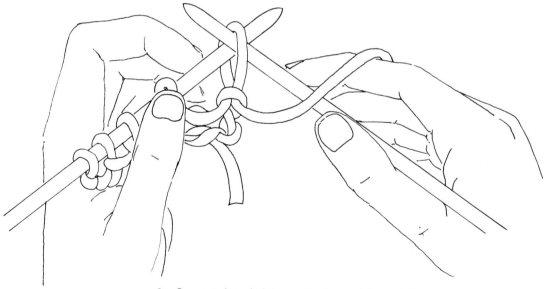

9 *Insert point of right needle from right to left*

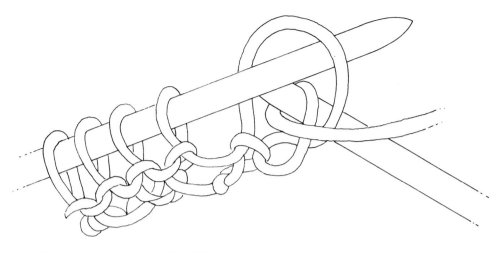

10 *Draw main yarn through left loop*

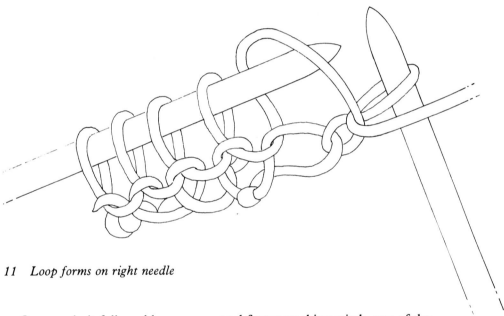

11 *Loop forms on right needle*

One row knit followed by one row purl forms stocking stitch, one of the most common patterns used in hand knitting. Good, even stocking stitch is essential when knitting in cotton yarns, particularly for large stretches of knitting, for example between garter-stitch ridges on bedspreads. If the stocking stitch appears to be marred by ridges, try experimenting by using a size finer needle for the purl rows – workers frequently purl more loosely than they knit.

Casting off
The directions here refer to casting off knitwise. It is sometimes more correct to cast off in pattern or rib, following the previous rows – this means knitting or purling the stitches before lifting them over and off the needle.

With the needles held as if to knit a row, work the first two stitches on to the right-hand needle. Using the point of the left needle, lift the first stitch knitted over the second stitch and off the right-hand needle. Knit the next stitch on to the right-hand needle and lift off the first stitch over the last stitch knitted. Continue in this manner along the row of stitches until just one stitch remains on the right-hand needle.

Draw out this stitch, cut the yarn to leave a long end and draw this end through the elongated stitch. Draw up tightly to secure.

Try to avoid casting off tightly unless specifically advised. Casting off has a tendency to draw in the edge anyway and a tight row could not only snap in wear but might produce problems in sewing up, since the cast-on edge is usually fairly loose and cast-off and cast-on edges are often joined together in household linens.

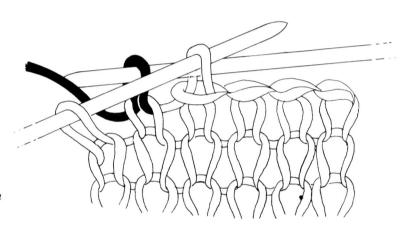

12   Work two stitches on to right needle

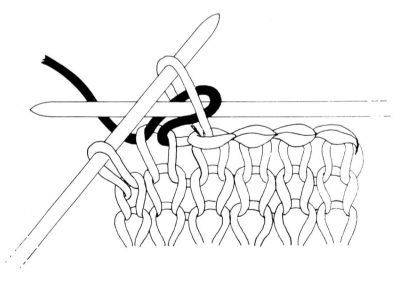

13   Lift first stitch over second stitch

Increasing

There are various methods of increasing in knitting, the most common method being simply to work twice into the following stitch. To do this, knit the next stitch in the usual way but do not let the old stitch slip off the left-hand needle. Instead, take the main yarn to the back of the work and knit into the back of the same loop and then take the old loop off the left-hand needle. Alternatively the second stitch taken from the original loop could be purled. In either case there are now two loops on the right-hand needle.

Another method of making a new stitch is to increase between stitches. Insert the point of the right-hand needle between the next two stitches, lift the loop lying between the stitches on to the left-hand needle, and knit or purl into the back of the loop. Care must be taken with this method since it does not require an actual stitch to make the increase. This particular method of increasing is always specified in the instructions, as failure to work the increase between the stitches will result in the pattern not working correctly across the row.

A decorative form of increasing is the simple 'yarn over'. This usually creates a hole on the right side of the work and is worked as follows. Take the main yarn round and over the needle before working the next stitch. On the following row, work this extra loop as a stitch. Some of the pattern instructions call for two loops to be formed before the following stitch – these will become two stitches on the next row and sometimes form a larger hole.

Decreasing

Decreases can be made at the beginning and end of rows and also in the middle. The most usual way to decrease is to work the next two stitches together. The decrease may be used to alter the actual size of the piece being worked or as decoration. Decorative decreases are specified in the pattern; for example, at one end of the motif you may be required to knit two stitches together and at the other, to knit a stitch, slip a stitch then using the point of the left-hand needle to lift the first stitch over the second. Occasionally two stitches will be decreased, either by working three stitches together by inserting the point of the right-hand needle through all three stitches on the left needle before knitting or purling, or by slipping one stitch, knitting the next two stitches together then lifting the slipped stitch over the last stitch on the right-hand needle. Stitches are also knitted or purled through the backs of the loops to produce a decorative effect.

Unless otherwise specified, when decreasing to alter the shaped pieces in the patterns, simply knit the next two stitches together.

Crochet stitches and methods

Crochet stitches are very easily formed and the same stitches may be used in a variety of ways, for all-over fabric, for decorative edgings and worked in rounds.

Making chain

Begin by making a slip knot as if for knitting. Draw this loop firmly on to the crochet hook. Hold the hook in the right hand and the yarn in the left hand. The yarn is slipped around the left hand as shown, and it will feed more comfortably into the hook if the ball of yarn is kept to the left of the worker (unlike knitting where it is more natural for the ball of yarn to be kept to the right of the worker).

Holding the hook and yarn, take the hook under the yarn (thus wrapping the yarn round the hook) and draw this loop forward and through the slip knot. One chain stitch has been made. Continue to wrap the yarn round the hook and draw loops through until the required number of chain has been made. After approximately five chain are made it is necessary to move down the chain that has been made. Hold the made chain firmly with the fingers of the left hand.

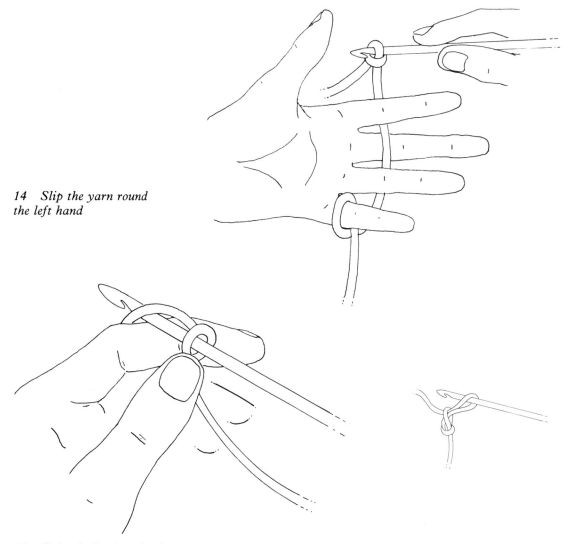

14 *Slip the yarn round the left hand*

15 *Take the hook under the yarn*

16 *Draw the loop through the slip knot*

Slip stitch

This stitch is seldom used as part of the actual pattern. It generally occurs in shaping garments and in joining rows or rounds of crochet.

Insert the hook under the *two* loops of the stitch instructed, wrap the yarn round the hook and draw the loop through.

Double crochet

Insert the hook into the next chain or the next stitch instructed, under the top *two* loops, wrap the yarn round the hook and draw the loop through, wrap the yarn round the hook again and draw through the two loops on the hook. One double crochet stitch has been made. This stitch may also be used to neaten edges by inserting the hook into the edge of the main crochet or knitting and forming double crochet stitches in the same way.

17 *Draw through two loops on hook*

Treble crochet

Before inserting the hook wrap the yarn round the hook, then insert the hook into the next chain or stitch instructed under the *two* top loops, wrap the yarn round the hook and draw it through the stitch (three loops on the hook). Wrap the yarn round the hook and draw through the first two loops on the hook, wrap the yarn round the hook once more and through the remaining two loops. One treble has been made. Continue in the same way across the row.

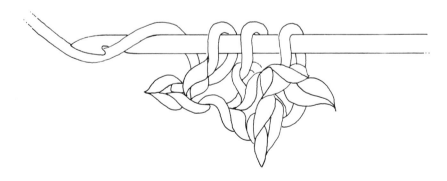

18 *Three loops on the hook*

Double treble

This stitch is a longer version of the treble. Wrap the yarn twice round the hook, insert the hook into the next stitch instructed, draw a loop through, yarn round hook and through the first two loops on the hook. Wrap and draw through two loops until one loop remains on the hook.

Half treble

This is a small version of treble that is sometimes used to form petals in Irish crochet. Wrap the yarn round the hook as if to treble, insert the hook, draw a loop through (three loops on the hook), yarn round hook and draw through all three loops together.

It is important to note that in crochet patterns it is frequently necessary to build up the depth of a row or round at its beginning, so a row may well start with a number of chain. If these chain are followed by the words 'miss one stitch' this indicates that the chain are to stand as the first stitch and should be counted and treated as a stitch on the following row or round.

Counting the rows

In both knitting and crochet the number of rows can be vital to the correct measurements. For knitting, row counters can be purchased – these slip on to the end of the knitting needle and it is a simple movement to record each row as it is worked. How can you remember to turn the counter? As each row is completed, the end of the left-hand needle slips through the left hand as the empty needle is transferred to the right hand; on every alternate row the needle with the row counter slips through in this way and the row counter touching the fingers serves as a reminder and should be turned at that very moment – note that two numbers need to be turned. This is far less trouble than marking numbers down in a notebook, although when working with four needles, or crochet, a written record of the rows is probably the safest method. Where squares are being made it is essential that exactly the same number of rows is worked for each to make the row-ends align for making up.

It is fairly easy to count rows of crochet but working in rounds usually requires the use of a marker to indicate the beginning and end of a round. Small plastic markers are now available and are recommended. These slip into the work with a twisting movement and, being plastic, they do not damage the work and are simple to remove when the article is finished.

Left-handed knitting and crochet

It is no more difficult for left-handed people to learn knitting and crochet than right-handed. The instructions should be followed but reversed by reading left for right and right for left. At the same time place a mirror by the book so that a reflection of the diagrams may be seen, showing the drawings in reverse.

Teaching the crafts

If you are teaching someone else to knit or crochet, use the instructions from the book. This is much easier for the learner than having to keep stopping to re-read the instructions. Read each part slowly and, for a right-handed learner, sit beside him or her. For the left-handed worker sit opposite to demonstrate – in this way your movements will be reflected.

Practice pieces

Tedious though it may seem, a few pieces must be made before attempting too complex an item. After learning the basic knit, purl and treble crochet, keeping a neat square and steady tension, turn to the particular pattern that you wish to make and consider whether there are any special stitches or techniques you will need in order to make that item. Just spend a little more time working a practice piece that incorporates those techniques. This will not only save time once you have embarked on a large project but could also prevent the misery of pulling out a piece of work and the possibility of a somewhat untidy area in your otherwise pristine white work.

Although some of the pattern stitches used in this book may appear complicated, all stitches are based on knit and purl, double crochet and treble crochet and any elaboration is explained in the pattern and very quickly learned. One of the great advantages of working in strips or squares is the speed, not only of working, but of learning the pattern, enabling the worker to knit or crochet without having constantly to refer to the book.

Except for the pram and cot covers, each item is worked in pure cotton. This is one of the easiest yarns to handle. It is smooth and retains its suppleness even in humid conditions, making it a perfect yarn with which to learn or refresh the memory while making these lovely old patterns.

If after looking at one of the articles in this book you feel tempted to learn or to return to knitting and crochet, be assured that after a few practice squares a novice may produce as accomplished an item as any experienced craftsman or woman. Your results will certainly be treasured in years to come.

Abbreviations

alt	alternate	ch	chain
approx	approximately	dc	double crochet
beg	begin(ning)	htr	half treble
cm	centimetre(s)	tr(s)	treble(s)
cont	continue	dtr	double treble
dec	decrease(ed)(ing)	sp	space
foll	following	yrh	yarn round hook
g	gram(s)		
in	inch(es)		
k	knit		
p	purl		
psso	pass slip stitch over		
rep	repeat		
sl st	slip stitch		
st(s)	stitch(es)		
st-st	stocking stitch		
tbl	through back of loop		
tog	together		
ybk	yarn back		
yfwd	yarn forward		
yrn	yarn round needle		

These are the abbreviations normally used in knitting and crochet patterns. Any special abbreviations are given in the text of the pattern.

Note on measurements

Only one size is given for each pattern. Where other sizes are required, calculations for measurements and quantities should be made individually (see page 9). Imperial measurements follow metric measurements in parentheses and are approximate. If you have trouble coping with metric measurements, use a modern tape measure with both types of measurements and convert the figures before working, making a note of all the measurements in your notebook.

The knitting patterns

One of the great attractions of the articles included in this section is that the result of our labour looks so intricate. There is no doubt that completing any of these patterns brings not only the satisfaction of a task well done but also the reward of praise from admirers. However, beginners need not feel that the designs are too complicated for them to work. So many of the finished pieces are made up of separate sections that after making one small part, even the novice will have practised any complex method sufficiently to carry on with the remaining patterns.

19   Octagon motif knitted bedspread, pattern 1

1   Octagon pattern bedspread

This design revives a romantic theme that is too beautiful to be hidden away for ever in old books of engravings. It has been termed 'Hungarian' but it could have come from almost anywhere. The shaped centre is octagonal and the spaces between form small squares. The sides have triangular shapes as fillers. The border is quite different in design but suits the gentle flow of the side edges and smoothly follows the rounded corners.

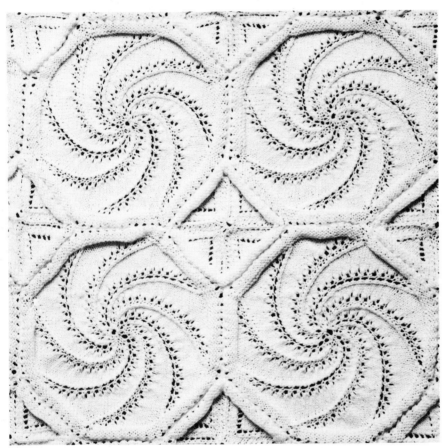

20   *Detail of knitted octagon and square infill motif, pattern 1*

Materials
36 balls (50 g) Twilley Stalite No 3 cotton
5 double-pointed 3¼ mm knitting needles

Measurements
152 cm (60 in) wide; 204 cm (80 in) long, excluding border

Tension
Each octagon measures 25 cm (10 in) across the centre.

Special abbreviation
M1   make 1 st by working yrn.

To make
Octagon panels   Make 48 pieces.
Cast on 8 sts (i.e. 2 sts on each of four needles and knit with the 5th needle).

Knit one round then continue in pattern thus:

1st round   *M1, k1; rep from * to end.
2nd round   K.
3rd round   *M1, k1; rep from * to end.
4th round   K.
5th round   *M1, k1, m1, k1, k2 tog; rep from * to end.
6th round   K.
7th round   *(M1, k1) 3 times, k2 tog; rep from * to end.
8th round   *K5, k2 tog; rep from * to end.
9th round   *(M1, k1) twice, m1, k2, k2 tog; rep from * to end.
10th round   *K6, k2 tog; rep from * to end.
11th round   *(M1, k1) twice, m1, k3, k2 tog; rep from * to end.
12th round   *K7, k2 tog; rep from * to end.
13th round   *(M1, k1) twice, m1, k4, k2 tog; rep from * to end.
14th round   *K8, k2 tog; rep from * to end.

Continue in this way, repeating the last 2 rounds, working 1 extra stitch before the 'k2 tog' in each repeat until the 35th round which will read:
*(M1, k1) twice, m1, k15, k2 tog; rep from * to end (*42 sts on each needle*).
36th round   *K19, k2 tog; rep from * to end.
37th and 38th rounds   P.
39th round   *P39, p twice in next st; rep from * to end.
40th and 41st rounds   P.
42nd round   *P1, (m1, p2 tog) to end along each needle.
Cast off very loosely.

Square motifs   Make 35 pieces.
Cast on 8 sts (i.e. 2 sts on each of four needles and knit with the 5th needle).

1st round   *M1, k1; rep from * to end.
2nd round and every foll alt round to 18th round   K to end.
3rd round   *M1, k3, m1, k1; rep from * to end.
5th round   *M1, k5, m1, k1; rep from * to end.
7th round   *M1, k2, k2 tog, m1, k3, m1, k1; rep from * to end.
9th round   *M1, k2, k2 tog, m1, k1, m1, sl1, k1, psso, k2, m1, k1; rep from * to end.

30

11th round   *M1, k2, k2 tog, m1, k3, m1, sl1, k1, psso, k2, m1, k1; rep from * to end.

13th round   *M1, k2, k2 tog, m1, k5, m1, sl1, k1, psso, k2, m1, k1; rep from * to end.

15th round   *M1, k2, k2 tog, m1, k7, m1, sl1, k1, psso, k2, m1, k1; rep from * to end.

17th round   *M1, k2, k2 tog, m1, k9, m1, sl1, k1, psso, k2, m1, k1; rep from * to end.

19th round   P to end.

20th round   P to end.

21st round   P to each corner and work k1, p1 in each corner st.

22nd and 23rd rounds   P to end.

24th round   *P1, (m1, p2 tog) to end along each needle.

Cast off very loosely.

Side triangle motifs Make 28 pieces.

With two 3¼ mm needles, cast on 1 st.

1st row   M1, k1, m1.

2nd row and every foll alt row to 24th row   P to end.

3rd row   K1, m1, k1, m1, k1.

5th row   K1, m1, k3, m1, k1.

7th row   K1, m1, k5, m1, k1.

9th row   K1, m1, k2, k2 tog, m1, k3, m1, k1.

11th row   K1, m1, k2, k2 tog, m1, k1, m1, sl1, k1, psso, k2, m1, k1.

13th row   K1, m1, k2, k2 tog, m1, k3, m1, sl1, k1, psso, k2, m1, k1.

15th row   K1, m1, k2, k2 tog, m1, k5, m1, sl1, k1, psso, k2, m1, k1.

17th row   K1, m1, k2, k2 tog, m1, k2, k2 tog, m1, k3, m1, sl1, k1, psso, k2, m1, k1.

19th row   K1, m1, k2, k2 tog, m1, k2, k2 tog, m1, k1, m1, sl1, k1, psso, k2, m1, sl1, k1, psso, k2, m1, k1.

21st row   K1, m1, k2, k2 tog, m1, k2, k2 tog, m1, k3, m1, sl1, k1, psso, k2, m1, sl1, k1, psso, k2, m1, k1.

23rd row   K1, m1, k2, k2 tog, m1, k2, k2 tog, m1, k5, m1, sl1, k1, psso, k2, m1, sl1, k1, psso, k2, m1, k1.

24th and 25th rows   P to end.

26th row   K to end.

27th row   P to end.

28th and 29th rows   Rep 26th and 27th rows.

30th row   P1, (m1, p2 tog) to end.

Cast off very loosely.

To make up

Back-stitch seam is most suitable for joining these motifs. With right sides of octagon motifs together sew the sections together, with six sections along the width and eight sections along the length, using just one-eighth of each side, thus leaving small square spaces between the octagons and triangle spaces at the sides. It is most convenient to join four octagons together first, then insert a square motif before moving on to the next set. When the twelve larger made-up pieces are completed join them into the finished bedspread. Finally sew in the triangle shapes to straighten the side edges.

2 Fluted border for octagon pattern bedspread

The fluted effect of this simple border is achieved by turning and working extra rows along some of the stitches. The pointed lace is knitted in with the main part of the border.

21 *Knitted fluted bedspread border, pattern 2*

Materials

11 balls (50 g) Twilley Stalite No 3 cotton
Pair 3¼ mm knitting needles

Measurements

Each strip approx 13 cm (5¼ in) wide
Two strips to measure approx 152 cm (60 in)
Two strips to measure approx 204 cm (80 in)

To make

Cast on 25 sts very loosely.

1st row K2, yrn, p2 tog, k16, yrn, p2 tog, k1, yfwd, k2.

2nd row K4, yrn, p2 tog, p16, yrn, p2 tog, turn.

3rd row Yrn, p2 tog, k16, yrn, p2 tog, k2, yfwd, k2.

4th row K5, yrn, p2 tog, p to last 4 sts, yrn, p2 tog, p2.

5th row K2, yrn, p2 tog, k16, yrn, p2 tog, k3, yfwd, k2.

6th row K6, yrn, p2 tog, p to last 4 sts, yrn, p2 tog, turn.

7th row Yrn, p2 tog, k16, yrn, p2 tog, k2 tog, (yrn) twice, k2, yfwd, k2.

8th row K6, p1 into second of 2 made loops of previous row, k1, yrn, p2 tog, p to last 4 sts, yrn, p2 tog, k2.

9th row K2, yrn, p2 tog, k16, yrn, p2 tog, k8.

10th row Cast off 5 sts loosely (1 st now on right-hand needle), k2, yrn, p2 tog, k2, (yrn, k2 tog) to last 4 sts, yrn, p2 tog, turn.

11th row Yrn, p2 tog, p16, yrn, p2 tog, k1, yfwd, k2.

12th row K4, yrn, p2 tog, k16, yrn, p2 tog, k2.

13th row K2, yrn, p2 tog, p16, yrn, p2 tog, k2, yfwd, k2.

14th row K5, yrn, p2 tog, k16, yrn, p2 tog, turn.

15th row Yrn, p2 tog, p16, yrn, p2 tog, k3, yfwd, k2.

16th row K6, yrn, p2 tog, k16, yrn, p2 tog, k2.

17th row K2, yrn, p2 tog, p16, yrn, p2 tog, k2 tog, (yrn) twice, k2, yfwd, k2.

18th row K6, p1 in second made loop of previous row, k1, yrn, p2 tog, k16, yrn, p2 tog, turn.

19th row Yrn, p2 tog, p16, yrn, p2 tog, k8.

20th row Cast off 5 sts loosely (1 st now on right-hand needle), k2, yrn, p2 tog, p2, (yrn, p2 tog) to last 2 sts, k2.

These 20 rows form the pattern. Continue in pattern until the straight edge, when slightly stretched fits along one side edge of the bedspread. Stitches may be either cast off or left with a long end to be grafted on to the adjacent cast-on edge. For a good fit it is advisable to tack the borders on before continuing work on the remaining sections.

To make up

Join the strips to the sides of the bedspread using the mattress seam method. Either graft the cast-off stitches to the cast-on stitches, or use fine back-stitch to sew these edges together. The extra rows worked to form the fluted effect will shape the corners of the border into a natural curve.

3 Leaf pattern bedspread

The raised leaf motif in the centre of joined squares is found in many traditional bedspreads, rugs, shawls and pram or cot covers. It can bring back waves of nostalgia for long-lost household treasures, but in general it is only the leaf motif that the articles have in common; the rest of the square can have enormous variations. This may be due to the fact that the patterns were copied in the past without the method being recorded and any deviation from the original pattern would be compounded every time another knitter embarked upon a new project.

22 *Leaf pattern knitted bedspread, pattern 3*

Materials
24 hanks (100 g) Twilley Handicraft No 1 cotton
Pair 3¾ mm knitting needles

Measurements

137 cm (54 in) wide; 182 cm (72 in) long, excluding border

Tension

Each square measures 23 cm (9 in) along each side edge.

Special abbreviation and note

M1 make 1 st by working yrn.

After the first two rows, all rows begin with a slip stitch.

In the pattern, all slipped stitches should be slipped purlwise (as if to purl the stitch but slip it on to the right-hand needle).

To make

Cast on 3 sts.

1st row (K1 and p1) both into 1st st, ybk, sl1, yfwd, (p1 and k1) both into last st.

2nd row (K1 and p1) both into 1st st, k1, p1, k1, (p1 and k1) both into last st (*7 sts*).

3rd row Sl1, k1, p3, k1, (p1 and k1) in last st.

4th row Sl1, k3, m1, k1, m1, k2, (p1 and k1) in last st.

5th row Sl1, k1, sl1, yfwd, p5, ybk, sl1, k1, (p1 and k1) in last st.

6th row Sl1, k5, m1, k1, m1, k4, (p1 and k1) in last st.

7th row Sl1, k1, sl1, k1, p7, k1, sl1, k1, (p1 and k1) in last st.

8th row Sl1, k7, m1, k1, m1, k6, (p1 and k1) in last st.

9th row Sl1, (k1, sl1) twice, p9, ybk, (sl1, k1) twice, (p1 and k1) in last st.

10th row Sl1, k9, m1, k1, m1, k8, (p1 and k1) in last st.

11th row Sl1, (k1, sl1) twice, k1, p11, (k1, sl1) twice, k1, (p1 and k1) in last st.

12th row Sl1, k11, m1, k1, m1, k10, inc as before in last st.

13th row Sl1, (k1, sl1) 3 times, p13, ybk, (sl1, k1) 3 times, inc in last st.

14th row Sl1, k13, m1, k1, m1, k12, inc in last st.

15th row Sl1, (k1, sl1) 3 times, k1, p15, (k1, sl1) 3 times, k1, inc in last st.

16th row Sl1, k8, sl1, k1, psso, k11, k2 tog, k7, inc in last st.

17th row Sl1, (k1, sl1) 4 times, p13, ybk, (sl1, k1) 4 times, inc in last st.

18th row Sl1, k9, sl1, k1, psso, k9, k2 tog, k8, inc in last st.

19th row (Sl1, k1) 5 times, p11, (k1, sl1) 4 times, k1, inc in last st.

20th row Sl1, k10, sl1, k1, psso, k7, k2 tog, k9, inc in last st.

21st row Sl1, (k1, sl1) 5 times, p9, ybk, (sl1, k1) 5 times, inc in last st.

22nd row Sl1, k11, sl1, k1, psso, k5, k2 tog, k10, inc in last st.

23rd row (Sl1, k1) 6 times, p7, (k1, sl1) 5 times, k1, inc in last st.

24th row Sl1, k12, sl1, k1, psso, k3, k2 tog, k11, inc in last st.

25th row Sl1, (k1, sl1) 6 times, p5, ybk, (sl1, k1) 6 times, inc in last st.

26th row Sl1, k13, sl1, k1, psso, k1, k2 tog, k12, inc in last st.

27th row (Sl1, k1) 7 times, p3, (k1, sl1) 6 times, k1, inc in last st.

28th row Sl1, k14, sl1, k2 tog, psso, k13, inc in last st (*31 sts*).

29th to 48th rows Continue by slipping the first st of every row and inc in last st of every row, keeping the (sl1, k1) pattern correct as previous rows.

49th row Sl1, p to last st, inc in last st.

50th row As 49th row.

51st row Sl1, k to last st, inc in last st.

52nd row As 49th row.

53rd row As 51st row (*56 sts*).

54th row Sl1, k1, m1, k2, k2 tog, *(sl1, k1, psso, k3, m1, k1, m1, k3, k2 tog) 4 times*, Sl1, k1, psso, k2, m1, k1, inc in last st.

55th row As 49th row.

56th row Sl1, k1, m1, k3, k2 tog, rep from * to * of 54th row, sl1, k1, psso, k3, m1, k1, inc in last st.

57th row As 49th row.

58th row Sl1, (k1, m1) twice, k3, k2 tog, rep from * to * of 54th row, sl1, k1, psso, k3, (m1, k1) twice, k1. *Do not* inc in last st.

59th row P to end. *Do not* inc in last st.

60th row Sl1, k2, m1, k1, m1, k3, k2 tog, rep from * to * of 54th row, sl1, k1, psso, k3, m1, k1, m1, k3.

61st row As 59th row.

62nd row Sl1, k3, m1, k1, m1, k3, k2 tog, rep from * to * of 54th row, sl1, k1, psso, k3, m1, k1, m1, k4.

63rd row As 59th row.

64th row Sl1, k4, m1, k1, m1, k3, k2 tog, rep from * to * of 54th row, sl1, k1, psso, k3, m1, k1, m1, k5.

65th and 66th rows P to end.

67th row K to end.

68th row P to end.

69th row Sl1, k65, k2 tog. This forms the first dec row.

70th row Sl1, k2, *(m1, sl1, k1, psso, k2)* 15 times, m1, sl1, k1, psso, k2 tog.

71st row Sl1, p to last 2 sts, p2 tog.

72nd row Sl1, rep from * to * of 70th row 15 times, m1, sl1, k1, psso, k2 tog.

73rd row As 71st row.

74th row Sl1, k2, rep from * to * of 70th row 14 times, m1, sl1, k1, psso, k2 tog.

75th, 76th and 77th rows As 71st row.

78th row Sl1, *(k2, k2 tog, m1)* 14 times, k2 tog.

79th row As 71st row.

80th row Sl1, rep from * to * of 78th row 13 times, k2, k2 tog.

81st row As 71st row.

82nd row Sl1, rep from * to * of 78th row 13 times, k2 tog.

83rd row As 71st row (*53 sts*).

84th row As 71st row.

85th row Sl1, k to last 2 sts, k2 tog.

86th row As 71st row.

87th and 88th rows As 85th row.

89th to 100th rows Beginning the rows with sl1 and ending with k2 tog, work these rows keeping the continuation of the sl1, k1 pattern as in 29th to 48th rows.

101st and 102nd rows Sl1, p to last 2 sts, p2 tog.

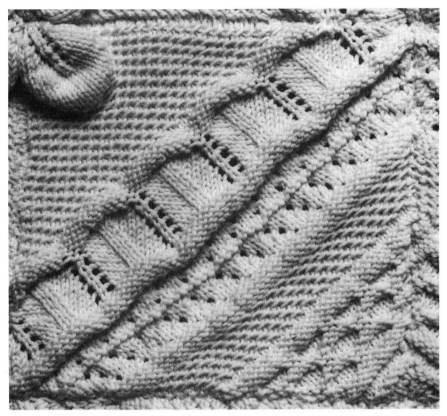

23   Detail of knitted leaf pattern square, pattern 3

103rd row   Sl1, k to last 2 sts, k2 tog.
104th row   As 101st row.
105th row   As 103rd row (*31 sts*).
106th row   Sl1, k1, (ybk, sl2, k4) 4 times, ybk, sl2, k1, k2 tog. Keep yarn
at back of work loose.
107th row   Sl1, p1, (sl2, p4) 4 times, sl2, p2 tog.
108th row   Sl1, (ybk, sl2, k4) 4 times, sl2, k2 tog.
109th row   Sl1, (sl2, p4) 4 times, sl1, p2 tog.
110th row   Sl1, p to last 2 sts, p2 tog.
111th row   Sl1, k to last 2 sts, k2 tog.
112th row   Sl1, k1, (ybk, sl2, k4) 3 times, ybk, sl2, k1, k2 tog.
113th row   Sl1, p1, (sl2, p4) 3 times, sl2, p2 tog.
114th row   Sl1, ybk, (sl2, k4, ybk) 3 times, sl2, k2 tog.
115th row   Sl1, (sl2, p4) 3 times, sl1, p2 tog.
116th row   Sl1, p to last 2 sts, p2 tog.
117th row   Sl1, k to last 2 sts, k2 tog (*19 sts*).
118th row   Sl1, k1, (ybk, sl2, k4) twice, ybk, sl2, k1, k2 tog.
119th row   Sl1, p1, (sl2, p4) twice, sl2, p2 tog.
120th row   Sl1, ybk, (sl2, k4) twice, ybk, sl2, k2 tog.
121st row   Sl1, (sl2, p4) twice, sl1, p2 tog.

122nd row   Sl1, p to last 2 sts, p2 tog.
123rd row   Sl1, k to last 2 sts, k2 tog.
124th and 125th rows   As 122nd row.
126th row   As 123rd row.
127th and 128th rows   As 122nd row.
129th and 130th rows   As 123rd row.
131st row   As 122nd row.
132nd row   As 123rd row.
133rd row   As 122nd row.
134th row   Sl1, k2 tog.
Cast off remaining 2 sts.
These 134 rows form a single square, working from one corner to the opposite diagonal corner.
Make a total of 48 squares.

To make up

These squares are best sewn together with a mattress seam, having the right side of the work facing so that each row can be joined almost invisibly. First join together four squares to form a larger square until twelve large squares have been completed. Join these large squares with three squares across the width and four squares to form the length.

4   Leaf pattern bedspread border

This is a neat border which takes up the raised leaf theme shown in the main part of the bedspread.

Materials

4 hanks (100 g) Twilley Handicraft No 1 cotton
Pair $3\frac{3}{4}$ mm knitting needles

Measurements

Each strip approx 12 cm ($4\frac{1}{2}$ in) wide
Two strips to measure approx 137 cm (54 in) each
Two strips to measure approx 182 cm (72 in) each

To make

Cast on 25 sts.
1st row   K3, k2 tog, yrn, p4, yfwd, k1, yrn, p4, yrn, p2 tog, p1, (yrn, p2 tog, k1) twice, yfwd, k2.

24   Knitted leaf pattern border, pattern 4

2nd row   P8, k8, p3, k9.

3rd row   K3, k2 tog, yrn, p4, yfwd, k3, yrn, p4, yrn, p2 tog, p2, (yrn, p2 tog, k1) twice, yfwd, k2.

4th row   P8, k9, p5, k9.

5th row   K3, k2 tog, yrn, p4, yfwd, k5, yrn, p4, yrn, p2 tog, p3, (yrn, p2 tog, k1) twice, yfwd, k2.

6th row   P8, k10, p7, k9.

7th row   K3, k2 tog, yrn, p4, yfwd, k7, yrn, p4, yrn, p2 tog, p4, (yrn, p2 tog, k1) twice, yfwd, k2.

8th row   P8, k11, p9, k9.

9th row   K3, k2 tog, yrn, p4, k3, sl1, k2 tog, psso, k3, p4, yrn, p2 tog, p5, (yrn, p2 tog, k1) twice, yfwd, k2.

10th row   P8, k12, p7, k9.

11th row   K3, k2 tog, yrn, p4, k2, sl1, k2 tog, psso, k2, p4, yrn, p2 tog, p6, (yrn, p2 tog, k1) twice, yfwd, k2.

12th row P8, k13, p5, k9.

13th row K3, k2 tog, yrn, p4, k1, sl1, k2 tog, psso, k1, p4, yrn, p2 tog, p7, (yrn, p2 tog, k1) twice, yfwd, k2.

14th row P8, k14, p3, k9.

15th row K3, k2 tog, yrn, p4, sl1, k2 tog, psso, p4, yrn, p2 tog, p8, (yrn, p2 tog, k1) twice, yfwd, k2.

16th row P8, k15, p1, k9.

17th row K3, k2 tog, yrn, p4, yfwd, k1, yrn, p4, yrn, p2 tog, p6, p2 tog, (yrn, k2 tog, k1) 3 times.

18th row P3, k1, p2, k1, p2, k13, p3, k9.

19th row K3, k2 tog, yrn, p4, yfwd, k3, yrn, p4, yrn, p2 tog, p5, p2 tog, (yfwd, k2 tog, k1) 3 times.

20th row P3, k1, p2, k1, p2, k12, p5, k9.

21st row K3, k2 tog, yrn, p4, yfwd, k5, yrn, p4, yrn, p2 tog, p4, p2 tog, (yfwd, k2 tog, k1) 3 times.

22nd row P3, k1, p2, k1, p2, k11, p7, k9.

23rd row K3, k2 tog, yrn, p4, yfwd, k7, yrn, p4, yrn, p2 tog, p3, p2 tog, (yfwd, k2 tog, k1) 3 times.

24th row P3, k1, p2, k1, p2, k10, p9, k9.

25th row K3, k2 tog, yrn, p4, k3, sl1, k2 tog, psso, k3, p4, yrn, p2 tog, p2, p2 tog, (yfwd, k2 tog, k1) 3 times.

26th row P3, k1, p2, k1, p2, k9, p7, k9.

27th row K3, k2 tog, yrn, p4, k2, sl1, k2 tog, psso, k2, p4, yrn, p2 tog, p1, p2 tog, (yfwd, k2 tog, k1) 3 times.

28th row P3, k1, p2, k1, p2, k8, p5, k9.

29th row K3, k2 tog, yrn, p4, k1, sl1, k2 tog, psso, k1, p4, yrn, p2 tog, p2 tog, (yfwd, k2 tog, k1) 3 times.

30th row P3, k1, p2, k1, p2, k7, p3, k9.

31st row K3, k2 tog, yrn, p4, sl1, k2 tog, psso, p4, yrn, sl1, p2 tog, psso, (yfwd, k2 tog, k1) 3 times.

32nd row P8, k7, p1, k9 (*25 sts*).

These 32 rows form the border pattern. Repeat them until strip, when slightly stretched, measures 137 cm (54 in). Cast off loosely.

Work another strip to this length, then work two more strips, each to be approx 182 cm (72 in) when slightly stretched. Cast off at end of each strip.

To make up

Using a mattress seam, join the strips to the side edges of the bedspread, fitting the strips right to the corners, plus approx 5 cm (2 in) overlap. When all four strips are sewn, fold back the overlap to the wrong side of the work to form a mitred corner. Using a mattress seam join the mitred corners, then neatly sew down the excess fabric to the wrong side of the work.

5 Canterbury bell bedspread

Little flower-shaped bells decorate this bedspread which truly lends itself to the cottage-garden image. The square motif, which is worked from corner to corner, was recorded as long ago as 1873.

25   *Knitted Canterbury bell pattern bedspread, pattern 5*

Materials
31 hanks (100 g) Twilley Handicraft No 1 cotton
Pair 4 mm knitting needles
3·5mm crochet hook

Measurements
152 cm (60 in) wide; 204 cm (80 in) long, excluding fringe

Tension

Each square measures 25 cm (10 in) along each side.

Special abbreviation and note

M1   make 1 st by working yrn.

Slip all slipped stitches knitwise unless otherwise stated.

To make

With 4 mm needles, cast on 1 st.

1st row   M1, k1.

2nd row   M1, k1, m1, k1.

3rd row   Sl1, k1, m1, k1, m1, k1.

4th row   K to end.

5th row   Sl1, k1, m1, k2, m1, k2.

6th row and foll alt rows to 18th row   Sl1, k to end.

7th row   Sl1, k1, m1, k4, m1, k2.

9th row   Sl1, k1, m1, k6, m1, k2.

11th row   Sl1, k1, m1, k8, m1, k2 (*14 sts*).

13th row   Sl1, k1, m1, p10, m1, k2.

15th row   Sl1, k1, m1, p12, m1, k2.

17th row   Sl1, k1, m1, p14, m1, k2.

19th row   Sl1, k1, m1, k16, m1, k2.

20th row   Sl1, k1, p18, k2.

21st row   Sl1, k1, m1, k18, m1, k2 (*24 sts*).

22nd row   Sl1, k to end.

23rd row   Sl1, k1, m1, p20, m1, k2.

24th row   Sl1, k to end.

25th row   Sl1, k1, m1, p22, m1, k2.

26th row   Sl1, k1, p24, k2.

27th row   Sl1, k1, m1, k24, m1, k2.

28th row   Sl1, k1, p26, k2.

29th row   Sl1, k1, m1, p26, m1, k2.

30th row   Sl1, k to end.

31st row   Sl1, k1, m1, p28, m1, k2.

32nd row   Sl1, k to end.

33rd row   Sl1, k1, m1, p30, m1, k2.

34th row   Sl1, k to end (*36 sts*).

35th row   Sl1, k1, m1, k2, *turn and cast on to right-hand needle 5 sts, turn, k3; rep from * 9 times more, m1, k2.

36th row   Sl1, k1, p4, *k5, p3; rep from * 9 times more, k2.

37th row   Sl1, k1, m1, k3, *p2 tog, p1, p2 tog, k3; rep from * 9 times more, k1, m1, k2.

38th row   Sl1, k1, p5, *k3, p1, p2 tog; rep from * ending last rep, k3, p4, k2.

39th row   Sl1, k1, m1, k4, *sl1 purlwise, p2 tog, psso, k2; rep from * 9 times more, k3, m1, k2.

40th row   Sl1, k1, p to last 2 sts, k2 (*43 sts*).

41st row   Sl1, k1, m1, k4, rep from * of 35th row 11 times, k5, m1, k2.

42nd row   Sl1, k1, p6, rep from * of 36th row 11 times, p3, k2.

43rd row   Sl1, k1, m1, k5, rep from * of 37th row 11 times, k3, m1, k2.

44th row   Sl1, k1, p7, rep from * of 38th row, ending last rep p6, k2.

45th row   Sl1, k1, m1, k6, rep from * of 39th row, ending last rep k7, m1, k2. (50)

46th row   As 40th row (*50 sts*).

47th row   Sl1, k1, m1, k6, rep from * of 35th row 12 times, ending last rep k7, m1, k2.

48th row   Sl1, k1, p8, rep from * of 36th row 12 times, ending last rep p7, k2.

49th row   Sl1, k1, m1, k7, rep from * of 37th row 12 times, ending last rep k8, m1, k2.

50th row   Sl1, k1, p9, rep from * of 38th row 12 times, ending last rep p8, k2.

51st row   Sl1, k1, m1, k8, rep from * of 39th row 12 times, ending last rep k9, m1, k2.

52nd row   As 40th row (*57 sts*).

53rd row   Sl1, k1, m1, p to last 2 sts, m1, k2.

54th row   Sl1, k to end.

55th row   Sl1, k1, m1, p to last 2 sts, m1, k2.

56th row   Sl1, k to end (*61 sts*).

57th row   Sl1, k1, m1, p3 tog, p to last 5 sts, p3 tog, m1, k2.

58th row   Sl1, k to end.

59th row   Sl1, k1, m1, p3 tog, p to last 5 sts, p3 tog, m1, k2 (*57 sts*).

60th row   Sl1, k1, p to last 2 sts, k2 (*57 sts*).

61st row   Sl1, k1, m1, k3 tog, k7, rep from * of 35th row 12 times, k4, k3 tog, m1, k2.

62nd row   Sl1, k1, p9, rep from * of 36th row, ending last rep p9, k2.

63rd row   Sl1, k1, m1, k3 tog, k6, rep from * of 37th row 12 times, k3, k3 tog, m1, k2.

64th row   Sl1, k1, p8, rep from * of 38th row 12 times, ending p5, k2.

65th row   Sl1, k1, m1, k3 tog, k4, rep from * of 39th row, k3, k3 tog, m1, k2.

66th row   As 40th row.

67th row   Sl1, k1, m1, k3 tog, k5, rep from * of 35th row 11 times, k3, k3 tog, m1, k2.

68th row   Sl1, k1, p8, rep from * of 36th row, p4, k2.

69th row   Sl1, k1, m1, k3 tog, k4, rep from * of 37th row, k2, k3 tog, m1, k2.

70th row   Sl1, k1, p7, rep from * of 38th row, p3, k2.

71st row   Sl1, k1, m1, k3 tog, k2, rep from * of 39th row, k2, k3 tog, m1, k2.

72nd row   Sl1, k1, p to last 2 sts, k2 (*45 sts*).

73rd row   Sl1, k1, m1, k3 tog, k3, rep from * of 35th row 10 times, k2, k3 tog, m1, k2.

74th row   Sl1, k1, p7, rep from * of 36th row, p2, k2.

75th row   Sl1, k1, m1, k3 tog, k2, rep from * of 37th row, k1, k3 tog, m1, k2.

76th row   Sl1, k1, p6, rep from * of 38th row, p1, k2.

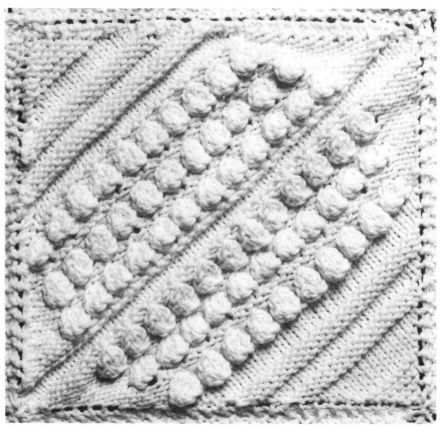

26 *Detail of Canterbury bell square, pattern 5*

77th row	Sl1, k1, m1, k3 tog, rep from * of 39th row, k1, k3 tog, m1, k2.
78th row	Sl1, k1, p to last 2 sts, k2.
79th row	Sl1, k1, m1, p3 tog, p to last 5 sts, p3 tog, m1, k2.
80th row	Sl1, k to end.
81st row	Sl1, k1, m1, p3 tog, p to last 5 sts, p3 tog, m1, k2.
82nd row	Sl1, k to end. 37
83rd row	Sl1, k1, m1, p3 tog, p to last 5 sts, p3 tog, m1, k2.
84th row	Sl1, k to end.
85th row	Sl1, k1, m1, k3 tog, k to last 5 sts, k3 tog, m1, k2.
86th row	Sl1, k1, p to last 2 sts, k2. 33
87th row	Sl1, k1, m1, k3 tog, k to last 5 sts, k3 tog, m1, k2.
88th row	Sl1, k to end. 33 31
89th row	Sl1, k1, m1, p3 tog, p to last 5 sts, p3 tog, m1, k2.
90th row	Sl1, k to end. 29
91st row	Sl1, k1, m1, p3 tog, p to last 5 sts, p3 tog, m1, k2.
92nd row	Sl1, k1, p to last 2 sts, k2. 27
93rd row	Sl1, k1, m1, k3 tog, k to last 5 sts, k3 tog, m1, k2.
94th row	Sl1, k1, p to last 2 sts, k2.
95th row	Sl1, k1, m1, p3 tog, p to last 5 sts, p3 tog, m1, k2.

13.99 = 1250

4.99 = 450

$$450\overline{)499}$$ ... 1.11
450
490
450
400

$$1250\overline{)3990}$$ ... 1.12
1250
1490
1250
240

the

are, using
e large
large
th.
net hook,
h tassel
lots of four
) below.
knot these
necessary.

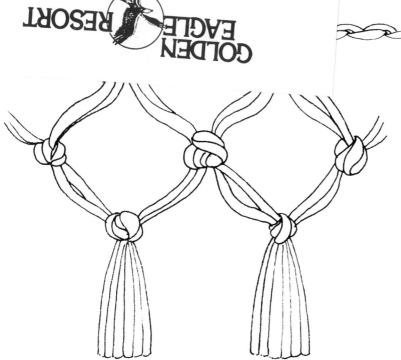

27　*Making a tasselled border*

6 Blackberry and smock pattern bedspread

This is a simple alternating patterned bedcover, the squares of which are worked vertically and rely on the texture of the traditional Aran patterns to provide character. Keep a close watch on the numbers of squares that you work or they may not line up for finishing as you want them to.

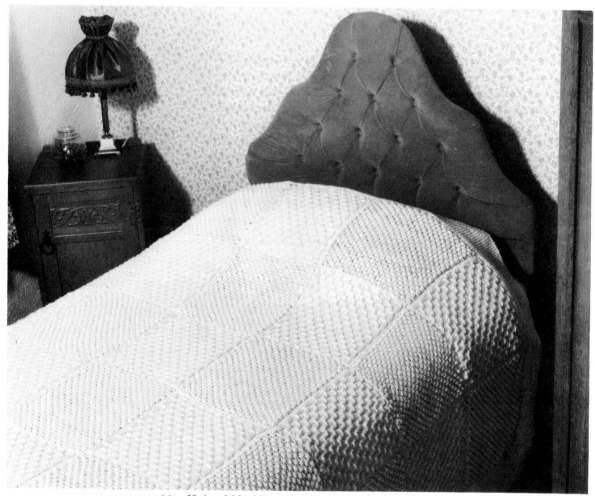

28 *Knitted blackberry and smock squares bedspread, pattern 6*

Materials
32 hanks (100 g) Twilley Handicraft No 1 cotton
Pair 4 mm knitting needles
Cable needle

Measurements

177 cm (70 in) along each side edge, excluding border

Tension

Each square measures 25 cm (10 in) along each side edge.

Blackberry pattern squares   Make 25 pieces.

Cast on 58 sts. Knit 1 row.
Continue in pattern thus:

1st row   (right side) K1, p to last st, k1.
2nd row   K1, *p3 tog, (k1, p1, k1) all in next st; rep from * to last st, k1.
3rd row   K1, p to last st, k1.
4th row   K1, *(k1, p1, k1) all in next st, p3 tog; rep from * to last st, k1.

These 4 rows form the pattern. Continue in pattern until work measures
25 cm (10 in), ending after 2nd or 4th pattern row.
Knit 1 row. Cast off.

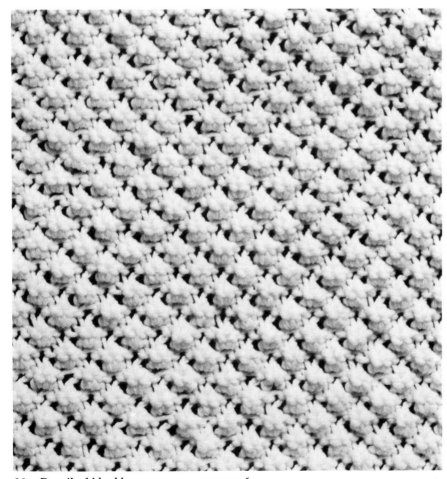

29   Detail of blackberry pattern, pattern 6

Smock pattern squares   Make 24 squares.

Cast on 76 sts.

1st row   (right side) K1, p2, *k2, p2; rep from * to last st, k1.

2nd row   K3, *p2, k2; rep from * to last st, k1.

3rd row   K1, p2, *slip next 6 sts on to cable needle, wind yarn 4 times clockwise round these sts then work (k2, p2, k2) into these sts, p2; rep from * to last st, k1.

4th row   As 2nd row.

5th and 6th rows   As 1st and 2nd rows.

7th row   K1, p2, k2, p2, *cable and wind yarn round next 6 sts as on 3rd row, p2; rep from * to last 5 sts, k2, p2, k1.

8th row   As 2nd row.

These 8 rows form the pattern. Continue in pattern until work measures 25 cm (10 in) ending after nearest 8th pattern row.

Cast off loosely.

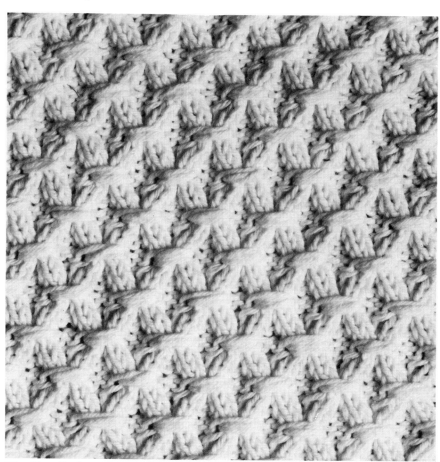

30   Detail of smock pattern, pattern 6

To make up

Form the squares into lines as indicated in the diagram on page 10. This will present a blackberry pattern square at each corner. The edges of the squares are best joined with a back-stitch seam, since the stitch and row numbers vary. For the neatest seaming, join the squares alternately into strips, then join the strips in one seam each.

7 Garter-stitch border

The very first knitting stitch that we learn is used here to make a smooth, flexible border for the blackberry and smock pattern bedspread. The borders may be worked in one continuous strip if desired, turning the corners as given and simply continuing along the following side. On the bedcover illustrated, the borders were made in four sections and grafted together after they were fitted to and sewn on to the main part.

The slipped stitch at the beginning of every row forms a neat, firm edge – this method is advisable for any garter-stitch work.

Materials
6 hanks (100 g) Twilley Handicraft No 1 cotton
Pair 4 mm knitting needles

Measurements
11 cm ($4\frac{1}{4}$ in) wide; approx 177 cm (70 in) long

Tension
21 sts and 34 rows to 10 cm (4 in)

To make
Cast on 22 sts, very loosely.
1st row K to end.
2nd row Sl1 knitwise, k to end.
Repeat 2nd row until strip, slightly stretched, measures the same as one side of bedspread.

To turn corner curve

1st row Sl1, k to last 2 sts, with yarn at back sl next st purlwise to right-hand needle, turn.
2nd row Ybk, sl the slipped st to right-hand needle, thus wrapping the yarn around the slipped st to avoid making a hole at the turn, k to end.
3rd row Sl1, k to last 4 sts, sl and wrap the next st as on 1st row, turn.
4th row As 2nd row.

5th row   Sl1, k to last 6 sts, sl and wrap the next st as on 1st row, turn.
6th row   As 2nd row.

Continue in this way until the row 'sl1, k1, sl and wrap the next st, turn' has been worked. Slip the slipped stitch back on to right-hand needle and knit to end. **

Repeat from the 1st row to ** twice more.

The work may be left on a spare needle for grafting or, if preferred, may continue along the second side. Where the work is continuous around all four sides, graft the stitches after the last corner to the cast-on edge. In all cases it is advisable to tack the border to the main part of the bedspread as it is worked to ensure a good fit.

If the border is worked as four equal strips, the corners may be grafted together or, if cast off, the ends of the strips should be neatly back-stitched together.

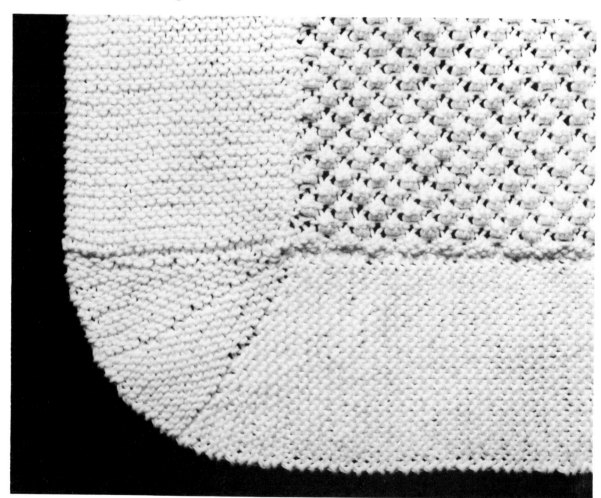

31   *Garter-stitch border detail, pattern 7*

8 Machine-worked bedspread

This design is also composed of small squares joined to make larger squares. The basic pattern is extremely simple, and experienced knitters could use this pattern as a basis for working more elaborate bedspreads.

The yarn used is relatively thick and a machine suitable for chunky yarns was used for the example shown here, but the principle would lend itself to almost any knitting machine. The squares are joined with double crochet to form a raised pattern for added interest and the edges are in crochet crab-stitch pattern.

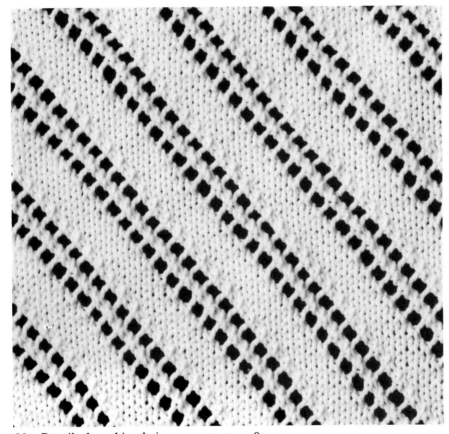

32 Detail of machine-knit square, pattern 8

Materials
28 hanks (100 g) Twilley Handicraft No 1 cotton
4 mm crochet hook
This bedspread was made on the **Bond knitting system**.

33 *Machine-worked bedspread, pattern 8*

Measurements

182 cm (72 in) wide; 243 cm (96 in) long

Tension

16 sts and 26 rows to 10 cm (4 in) in pattern using Keyplate 2

Square 1   Make 24 pieces.

Using closed-edge method, cast on 52 sts.
Knit 3 rows, ending carriage on right.
Continue in pattern thus:
1st row   Beg. at right-hand side, miss 4 sts, *(miss 1 st, transfer next st to missed needle at right-hand side) twice, miss 4 sts*; rep from * to * across the row, leaving empty needles in working position with latches open, k the row.
2nd row and foll alt rows   K the row.
3rd row   Miss 3 sts, rep from * to * of 1st row, leaving empty needles in working position with latches open, k the row.
5th row   Miss 2 sts, rep from * to * of 1st row across the row, leaving empty needles in working position with latches open, k the row.
Continue in this way, moving the pattern diagonally to the right until 78 pattern rows have been worked and joining new stitches into pattern as soon as possible at left-hand side.
Knit 3 rows. Cast off.

Square 2   Make 24 pieces.

Work as square 1, reversing the direction of the diagonal pattern thus:
1st row   Beg at left-hand side, miss 4 sts, *(miss 1 st, transfer next st to last missed st at left-hand side) twice, miss 4 sts*; rep from * to * across the row, leaving empty needles in working position with latches open, k the row.

To make up

With wrong sides together of one square 1 and one square 2, using crochet hook, *insert hook through both layers of fabric, draw loop through, yrh and through loops on hook; rep from * to end of side. Fasten off. Work the next two corresponding squares together in the same way. Using the same double-crochet method work the two sets of two squares together. Next join these larger squares together with double crochet, with three large squares across the width. Finally join the four strips of three squares with double crochet.

   To work the crab-stitch edging (see Fig. 34), work 1 row of double crochet all round the outer edge of the bedspread, working 3 double crochet in each corner; *do not turn*. To form the crab stitch, work 1 double crochet in each double crochet, working from left to right. Join with slip stitch to first double crochet. Fasten off.

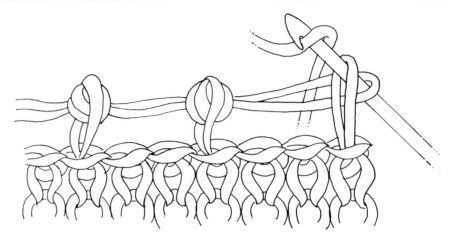

34 *Crab-stitch crochet edging*

9 Lace and moss stitch pattern tablecloth

This tablecloth will bring images of ladies with time on their hands, time to work beautiful articles and time to appreciate handmade linens. With the labour-saving devices available today, many of us can find time to create lovely things for the home and we can be secure in the knowledge that they will outlast many of the machine-made goods and will be popular with generations to come.

The cloth is worked in one piece, on quite a large number of stitches, but in this case when the first square is finished, the whole cloth will be finished. The lace diamond pattern is given first and is referred to throughout the pattern instructions. Once these few rows have been accomplished the knitting will become relatively simple.

Materials
17 balls (25 g) Twilley Crysette Super No 3 cotton
Pair $3\frac{1}{4}$ mm knitting needles

Measurements
Approx 91 cm (36 in.) along each side

Tension
24 sts to 10 cm (4 in) in pattern

35   *Knitted lace and moss stitch tablecloth, pattern 9*

Special abbreviations
M2   make two stitches by winding yarn twice round the needle. Note that each loop is worked separately on the following row.

Diamond pattern
1st row   *K5, k2 tog, m2, k2 tog, k4*.
2nd row   *P7, k1, p5*.
3rd row   *K3, (k2 tog, m2, k2 tog) twice, k2*.
4th row   *P5, k1, p3, k1, p3*.
5th row   *K1, (k2 tog, m2, k2 tog) 3 times*.
6th row   *(P3, k1) 3 times, p1*.
7th row   As 3rd row.
8th row   As 4th row.
9th row   As 1st row.
10th row   As 2nd row.

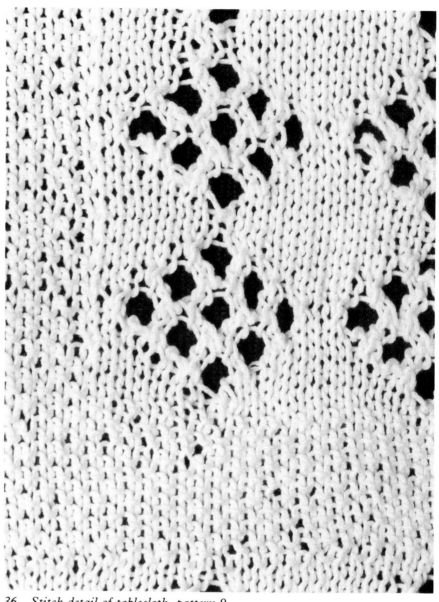

36   *Stitch detail of tablecloth, pattern 9*

To make

Cast on 220 sts.

Continue in moss stitch thus:

1st row   *K1, p1; rep from * to end.

2nd row   *P1, k1; rep from * to end.

These 2 rows form the moss stitch pattern. Repeat them until work measures 4 cm (1½ in). Now continue in diamond pattern with moss stitch borders at each end of row, placing stitches thus:

**1st row*   Moss st 12 sts, k to last 12 sts, moss st 12.

2nd row   Moss st 12 sts, p to last 12 sts, moss st 12.

3rd row   Moss st 12 sts, work from * to * of 1st diamond patt row to last 13 sts, k1, moss st 12.

4th row   Moss st 12 sts, work from * to * of 2nd diamond patt row to last 13 sts, p1, moss st 12.

Continue in this way, working subsequent diamond pattern rows until the 12th row has been completed which reads:

Moss st 12 sts, work from * to * of 10th diamond patt row to last 13 sts, p1, moss st 12.

13th and 14th rows   As 1st and 2nd rows.**

The work now continues with two outer moss stitch borders having a diamond panel between.

***15th row*   Moss st 12 sts, k14, moss st to last 26 sts, k14, moss st 12.

16th row   Moss st 12 sts, p14, moss st to last 26 sts, p14, moss st 12.

17th row   Moss st 12 sts, work from * to * of 1st diamond patt row over next 13 sts, k1, moss st to last 26 sts, work from * to * of 1st diamond patt row over next 13 sts, k1, moss st 12.

18th row   Moss st 12 sts, work from * to * of 2nd diamond patt row over next 13 sts, p1, moss st to last 26 sts, work from * to * of 2nd diamond patt row over next 13 sts, p1, moss st 12.

19th row   Moss st 12 sts, work from * to * of 3rd diamond patt row over next 13 sts, k1, moss st to last 26 sts, work from * to * of 3rd diamond patt row over next 13 sts, k1, moss st 12.

20th row   Moss st 12 sts, work from * to * of 4th diamond patt row over next 13 sts, p1, moss st to last 26 sts, work from * to * of 4th diamond patt row over next 13 sts, p1, moss st 12.

21st row   Moss st 12 sts, work from * to * of 5th diamond patt row over next 13 sts, k1, moss st to last 26 sts, work from * to * of 5th diamond patt row over next 13 sts, k1, moss st 12.

22nd row   Moss st 12 sts, work from * to * of 6th diamond patt row over next 13 sts, p1, moss st to last 26 sts, work from * to * of 6th diamond patt row over next 13 sts, p1, moss st 12.

23rd row   As 19th row.

24th row   As 20th row.

25th row   As 17th row.

26th row   As 18th row.

27th row   As 15th row.

28th row   As 16th row.***

The work will now have diamond patterns across the centre and between the moss stitch borders. Continue thus:

1st row   Moss st 12 sts, k14, moss st 12, k144, moss st 12, k14, moss st 12.

2nd row   Moss st 12 sts, p14, moss st 12, p144, moss st 12, p14, moss st 12.

3rd row   Moss st 12, work from * to * of 1st diamond patt row across next 13 sts, k1, moss st 12, work from * to * of 1st diamond patt row across centre 143 sts, k1, moss st 12, work from * to * across next 13 sts, k1, moss st 12.

4th row   Moss st 12, work from * to * of 2nd diamond patt row across next 13 sts, p1, moss st 12, work from * to * of 2nd diamond patt row across centre 143 sts, p1, moss st 12, work from * to * of 2nd diamond patt row across next 13 sts, p1, moss st 12.

5th row Moss st 12, work from * to * of 3rd diamond patt row across next 13 sts, k1, moss st 12, work from * to * of 3rd diamond patt row across centre 143 sts, k1, moss st 12, work from * to * of diamond patt row across next 13 sts, k1, moss st 12.

6th row Moss st 12, work from * to * of 4th diamond patt row across next 13 sts, p1, moss st 12, work from * to * of 4th diamond patt row across centre 143 sts, p1, moss st 12, work from * to * of 4th diamond patt row across next 13 sts, p1, moss st 12.

7th row Moss st 12, work from * to * of 5th diamond patt row across next 13 sts, k1, moss st 12, work from * to * of 5th diamond patt row across centre 143 sts, k1, moss st 12, work from * to * of 5th diamond patt row across next 13 sts, k1, moss st 12.

8th row Moss st 12, work from * to * of 6th diamond patt row across next 13 sts, p1, moss st 12, work from * to * of 6th diamond patt row across centre 143 sts, p1, moss st 12, work from * to * of 6th diamond patt row across next 13 sts, p1, moss st 12.

9th row Moss st 12, work from * to * of 7th diamond patt row across next 13 sts, k1, moss st 12, work from * to * of 7th diamond patt row across centre 143 sts, k1, moss st 12, work from * to * of 7th diamond patt row across next 13 sts, k1, moss st 12.

10th row Moss st 12, work from * to * of 8th diamond patt row across next 13 sts, p1, moss st 12, work from * to * across centre 143 sts, p1, moss st 12, work from * to * of 8th diamond patt row across next 13 sts, p1, moss st 12.

11th row Moss st 12, work from * to * of 9th diamond patt row across next 13 sts, k1, moss st 12, work from * to * of 9th diamond patt row across centre 143 sts, k1, moss st 12, work from * to * of 9th diamond patt row across next 13 sts, k1, moss st 12.

12th row Moss st 12, work from * to * of 10th diamond patt row across next 13 sts, p1, moss st 12, work from * to * of 10th diamond patt row across centre 143 sts, p1, moss st 12, work from * to * of 10th diamond patt row across next 13 sts, p1, moss st 12.

13th and 14th rows Rep 1st and 2nd of these last rows. Repeat the last 14 rows until work measures approx 76 cm (30 in), ending after nearest 14th row.

Now repeat from *** to ***, then repeat from ** to **.

Work in moss stitch for 4 cm (1½ in) to match beginning of cloth.

Cast off firmly.

To complete

Darn in ends neatly along side edges.

Should the work require pressing, pass the iron only lightly over the work to avoid flattening the texture of the pattern. Dressing the fabric (see page 13) is particularly suitable for this item.

10   Lace swirl table linen

This set of large centre mat, place mats and coasters is worked mainly in stocking stitch. The swirl effect is achieved by turning and knitting extra rows over a calculated number of stitches. The same principle is followed over all the pieces and the pointelle lace-edged borders are worked in with the main sections.

Materials

8 balls (25 g) Twilley Lyscordet No 5 cotton
This quantity will make a centre mat, four place mats and four coasters; for separate items:
Centre mat, 2 balls Twilley Lyscordet
Four place mats, 3 balls Twilley Lyscordet
Four coasters, 3 balls Twilley Lyscordet
Pair 3 mm knitting needles

Measurements

Large mat, 38 cm (15 in) in diameter
Place mats, 23 cm (9 in) in diameter
Coasters, 15 cm (6 in) in diameter

Tension

30 sts and 38 rows to 10 cm (4 in) measured over stocking stitch

To make
The centre mat

Cast on 45 sts, loosely, and slip all slipped sts purlwise.

1st row   Sl1, k39, yrn, p2 tog, k1, yfwd, k2.
2nd row   K4, yrn, p2 tog, p38, turn, leaving 2 sts.
3rd row   Sl1, k37, yrn, p2 tog, k2, yfwd, k2.
4th row   K5, yrn, p2 tog, p36, turn, leaving 4 sts.
5th row   Sl1, k35, yrn, p2 tog, k3, yfwd, k2.
6th row   K6, yrn, p2 tog, p34, turn, leaving 6 sts.
7th row   Sl1, k33, yrn, p2 tog, k2 tog, (yrn) twice, k2, yfwd, k2.
8th row   K6 p1 into second of two made loops on 7th row, k1, yrn, p2 tog, p32, turn, leaving 8 sts.
9th row   Sl1, k31, yrn, p2 tog, k8.
10th row   Cast off 5 sts loosely (1 st now on right-hand needle), k2, yrn, p2 tog, p30, turn, leaving 10 sts.
11th row   Sl1, k29, yrn, p2 tog, k1, yfwd, k2.
12th row   K4, yrn, p2 tog, p28, turn.
13th row   Sl1, k27, yrn, p2 tog, k2, yfwd, k2.
14th row   K5, yrn, p2 tog, p26, turn.

37 *Circular lace swirl knitted table linen, pattern 10*

15th row Sl1, k25, yrn, p2 tog, k3, yfwd, k2.

16th row K6, yrn, p2 tog, p24, turn.

17th row Sl1, k23, yrn, p2 tog, k2 tog, (yrn) twice, k2, yfwd, k2.

18th row K6, p1 into second made loop of previous row, k1, yrn, p2 tog, p22, turn.

19th row Sl1, k21, yrn, p2 tog, k8.

20th row Cast off 5 sts loosely (1 st now on right-hand needle), k2, yrn, p2 tog, p20, turn.

Continue in this way, working 2 sts less before turning on wrong-side rows until the 39th row has been worked.

40th row Cast off 5 sts loosely (1 st now on right-hand needle), k2, yrn, p2 tog, p2, (yrn, p2 tog) to last 2 sts, p2.

These 40 rows form one pattern repeat. Work 7 more repeats of the 40-row pattern to form a complete circle. The stitches may be cast off and seamed to the cast-on edge but grafting is recommended for the join, so as to imply continuous knitting.

To complete

If the seam is to be grafted, do not cast off the stitches but leave with a long end. If the stitches have been cast off, use mattress seam with the right side of the work facing to sew the cast-off and cast-on edges together, aligning the stitches as closely as possible.

The place mats

Cast on 25 sts loosely and slip all slipped sts purlwise.

1st row Sl1, k19, yrn, p2 tog, k1, yfwd, k2.

2nd row K4, yrn, p2 tog, p18, turn, leaving 2 sts.

3rd row Sl1, k17, yrn, p2 tog, k2, yfwd, k2.

4th row K5, yrn, p2 tog, p16, turn, leaving 4 sts.

5th row Sl1, k15, yrn, p2 tog, k3, yfwd, k2.

6th row K6, yrn, p2 tog, p14, turn, leaving 6 sts.

7th row Sl1, k13, yrn, p2 tog, k2 tog, (yrn) twice, k2, yfwd, k2.

8th row K6, p1 into second loop of two made loops on 7th row, k1, yrn, p2 tog, p12, turn.

9th row Sl1, k11, yrn, p2 tog, k8.

10th row Cast off 5 sts loosely (1 st now on right-hand needle), k2, yrn, p2 tog, p10, turn.

11th row Sl1, k9, yrn, p2 tog, k1, yfwd, k2.

12th row K4, yrn, p2 tog, p8, turn.

13th row Sl1, k7, yrn, p2 tog, k2, fwd, k2.

14th row K5, yrn, p2 tog, p6, turn.

15th row Sl1, k5, yrn, p2 tog, k3, yfwd, k2.

16th row K6, yrn, p2 tog, p4, turn.

17th row Sl1, k3, yrn, p2 tog, k2 tog, (yrn) twice, k2, yfwd, k2.

18th row K6, p1 into second loop of two made loops of previous row, k1, yrn, p2 tog, p2, turn.

19th row Sl1, k1, yrn, p2 tog, k8.

20th row Cast off 5 sts loosely (1 st now on right-hand needle), k2, yrn,

p2 tog, p2, (yrn, p2 tog) 8 times, p2.
These 20 rows form one pattern repeat. Work 11 more repeats of the
20-row pattern to form a complete circle.

To complete
Cast off stitches or leave to graft and complete as instructed for the centre
mat.

38   Knitted place mat of table linen, pattern 10

The coasters
Cast on 15 sts loosely and slip all slipped sts purlwise.
1st row   Sl1, k9, yrn, p2 tog, k1, yfwd, k2.
2nd row   K4, yrn, p2 tog, p8, turn, leaving 2 sts.
3rd row   Sl1, k7, yrn, p2 tog, k2, yfwd, k2.
4th row   K5, yrn, p2 tog, p6, turn, leaving 6 sts.
5th row   Sl1, k5, yrn, p2 tog, k3, yfwd, k2.
6th row   K6, yrn, p2 tog, p4, leaving 6 sts.
7th row   Sl1, k3, yrn, p2 tog, k2 tog, (yrn) twice, k2, yfwd, k2.

8th row   K6, p1 in second loop of two made loops of previous row, k1, yrn, p2 tog, p2, turn, leaving 8 sts.

9th row   Sl1, k1, yrn, p2 tog, k8.

10th row   Cast off 5 sts loosely (1 st now on right-hand needle), k2, yrn, p2 tog, (yrn, p2 tog) 3 times, p2.

These 10 rows form one pattern repeat. Work 15 more repeats of the 10-row pattern to form a complete circle.

To complete

Cast off stitches or leave to graft and complete as instructed for the centre mat.

11   Pleated teacosy

39   Pleat-knitted teacosy, pattern 11

Most of us are familiar with this garter-stitch cosy. Sometimes it is worked in alternate colours but this example is worked in thick white cotton throughout. Cotton serves as splendid insulation and the cosy will wash and wear well.

A pompon completes the top but a crochet or knitted loop at the top will serve as a hanger when the cosy is not in use.

Materials
2 hanks (100 g) Twilley Handicraft No 1 cotton
Pair 4 mm knitting needles

Tension
The stocking-stitch tension is 20 sts and 24 rows to 10 cm (4 in). If you obtain that tension in stocking stitch your tension will be correct for this pattern.

Note
Wind each hank into a ball and label one ball A and one ball B.
Make two pieces.
With ball A, cast on 98 sts.
Work 6 rows garter stitch (every row knit).
Continue in garter stitch as follows, working the pleats by carrying yarn not in use tightly across the back of the work.
1st row K 1A, (8B, 8A) to last st, 1B.
2nd row Twisting yarns at beg of row to avoid leaving holes, K 1B, (8A, 8B) to last st, 1A.
Repeat last 2 rows until work measures 17 cm (6½ in) ending after a wrong-side row.

Shape top
1st row K 1A, (with B, k2 tog, k4, k2 tog, with A, k2 tog, k4, k2 tog) to last st, k 1B.
2nd row K 1B, (6A, 6B) to last st, 1A.
3rd row K 1A, (with B, k2 tog, k2, k2 tog, with A, k2 tog, k2, k2 tog) to last st, 1B.
4th row K 1B, (4A, 4B) to last st, 1A.
5th row K 1A, (with B, k2 tog twice, with A, k2 tog twice) to last st 1B.
6th row K 1B, (2A, 2B) to last st, 1A.
7th row K 1A, (k2 tog B, k2 tog A) to last st, 1B.
Thread remaining stitches on to 2 strands of yarn and pull up to tighten. Fasten off securely, leaving a long end.

To make up
Join the side seams leaving approx 10 cm (4 in) free for the teapot handle and spout, each opening to be approx 4 cm (1½ in) from cast-on edge.

Use remaining yarn to form a pompon and sew the pompon to the top to conceal the join.

If preferred a small loop may be made thus: cast on 20 sts. Cast off the sts. Fasten off. Join the two ends to form a circle and sew to the top of the cosy.

12   Bedlinen edgings

40   Knitted edging for bedlinen, pattern 12

Just a very little time and expense can transform your bedlinen into something to treasure. Adding handwork to bedlinen is no longer an old-fashioned thing to do – the standards of our forebears are now appreciated again and all types of crafts are treated with great respect.

One pattern decorates the linen in the photograph, and two alternatives are suggested. There are many more patterns for this type of edging and most of them use a few stitches and rows, making it a simple task and one that can be conveniently carried around so that a few more rows may be added when a moment arises.

Materials

2 balls (25 g) Twilley Lyscordet No 5 cotton to make sheet edging (see measurements)
2 balls to make one pillowslip edging
Pair 2¾ mm knitting needles

Measurements

8 cm (3 in) wide; sheet edging 182 cm (72 in) long; each pillowslip 102 cm (40 in) long

Tension

Knitting needles should be used with this yarn to produce strips with a width of 8 cm (3 in).

To make

Cast on 17 sts.
Foundation row Sl1, k2, yfwd, (k2 tog) twice, k2, k2 tog, yfwd, k3, yfwd, k1, yfwd, k2. This row is not repeated.
1st row Yrn, k2 tog, k1, p10, k2, yfwd, k2 tog, k1.
2nd row Sl1, k2, yfwd, k2 tog, (k2, k2 tog, yfwd) twice, k3, yfwd, k2.
3rd row Yrn, k2 tog, k1, p11, k2, yrn, k2 tog, k1.
4th row Sl1, k2, yfwd, k2 tog, k1, k2 tog, yfwd, k2, k2 tog, yfwd, k5, yfwd, k2.
5th row Yrn, k2 tog, k1, p12, k2, yfwd, k2 tog, k1.
6th row Sl1, k2, yfwd, (k2 tog) twice, yfwd, k2, k2 tog, yfwd, k3, yfwd, k2 tog, k2, yfwd, k2.
7th row Yrn, k2 tog, k1, p13, k2, yfwd, k2 tog, k1.
8th row Sl1, k2, yfwd, k2 tog, k3, k2 tog, yfwd, k3, (yfwd, k2 tog) twice, k2, yfwd, k2.
9th row Yrn, k2 tog, k1, p14, k2, yfwd, k2 tog, k1.
10th row Sl1, k2, yfwd, k2 tog, k2, k2 tog, yfwd, k3, (yfwd, k2 tog) 3 times, k2, yfwd, k2.
11th row Yrn, k2 tog, k1, p15, k2, yfwd, k2 tog, k1.
12th row Sl1, k2, yfwd, k2 tog, k1, k2 tog, yfwd, k1, yfwd, sl1, k1, psso, k2, (yfwd, k2 tog) twice, k1, k2 tog, yfwd, k2 tog, k1.
13th row As 9th row.
14th row Sl1, k2, yfwd, (k2 tog) twice, yfwd, k3, yfwd, sl1, k1, psso, k2,

yfwd, k2 tog, k1, k2 tog, yfwd, k2 tog, k1.

15th row   As 7th row.

16th row   Sl1, k2, yfwd, k2 tog, k3, k2 tog, yfwd, k1, yfwd, sl1, k1, psso, k3, k2 tog, yfwd, k2 tog, k1.

17th row   As 5th row.

18th row   Sl1, k2, yfwd, k2 tog, k2, k2 tog, yfwd, k3, yfwd, sl1, k1, psso, k1, k2 tog, yfwd, k2 tog, k1.

19th row   As 3rd row.

20th row   Sl1, k2, yfwd, k2 tog, k1, k2 tog, yfwd, k2, k2 tog, yfwd, k1, yfwd, sl1, k2 tog, psso, yfwd, k2 tog, k1.

21st row   As 1st row.

22nd row   Sl1, k2, yfwd, (k2 tog) twice, k2, k2 tog, yfwd, k3, yfwd, k1, yfwd, k2 tog, k1 (*18 sts*).

These 22 rows form the pattern. Repeat them until work fits, unstretched, along width of sheet or all round pillowslip opening. Cast off.

To complete

Sew neatly to sheet edge or pillowslip opening. On pillowslip opening, join the cast-on edge to the cast-off edge.

41   *Detail of knitted bedlinen edging, pattern 12*

13 Alternative linen edgings

Materials
These will be similar to the linen edging requirements listed above for pattern 12.

Measurements
The fan pattern edging is 5 cm (2 in) wide.
The clover pattern edging is 6 cm (2½ in) wide.
The length of the edging is optional.

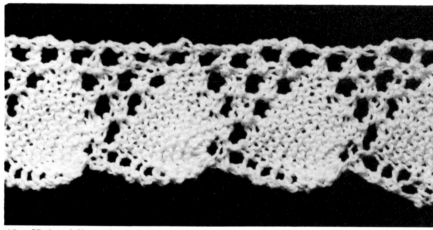

42 *Knitted linen fan edging, pattern 13*

To make fan edging
Cast on 14 sts.

1st row Sl1, (yrn) twice, k2 tog, k9, yrn, p2 tog.
2nd row K13, p1, k1.
3rd row Sl1, k12, yrn, p2 tog.
4th row K15.
5th row Sl1, *(yrn) twice, k2 tog; rep from * once more, k8, yrn, p2 tog.
6th row K12, p1, k2, p1, k1.
7th row Sl1, k14, yrn, p2 tog.
8th row K17.
9th row Sl1, *(yrn) twice, k2 tog; rep from * twice more, k8, yrn, p2 tog.
10th row K12, p1, (k2, p1) twice, k1.
11th row Sl1, k17, yrn, p2 tog.
12th row K20.
13th row K2 tog, *(yrn) twice, k2 tog; rep from * 3 times more, k8, yrn, p2 tog.
14th row K12, p1, (k2, p1) 3 times, k1.
15th row Sl1, k12, *insert right-hand needle point through the 2nd st on

left-hand needle and lift the st over the first st and off the needle; rep from * until 9 sts have been lifted over the same st, k1.

16th row   K14.

These 16 rows form the pattern. Repeat them until the strip is the required length.

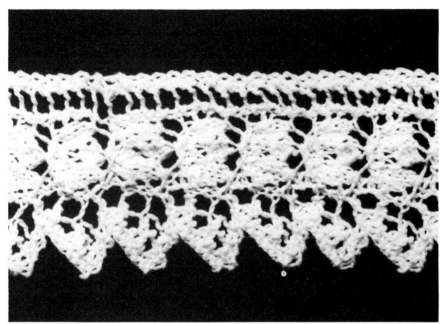

43   Knitted linen clover edging, pattern 13

To make clover pattern edging

Cast on 12 sts.

1st row   Sl1, k2 tog, (yrn) twice, k2 tog, yrn, k1, yrn, (k1, p1, k1) all in next st, (yfwd, k1) twice, (yrn) twice, k2 tog, k1.

2nd row   K3, p1, k1, p9, k2, p1, k2.

3rd row   Sl1, k2 tog, (yrn) twice, k2 tog, (yfwd, k3) 3 times, yfwd, *k1, (yrn) twice; rep from * once more, k2 tog, k1.

4th row   K3, p1, k2, p1, k1, p5, p3 tog, p5, k2, p1, k2.

5th row   Sl1, k2 tog, (yrn) twice, k2 tog, (yrn, sl1, k1, psso, k1, k2 tog, yrn, k1) twice, * (yrn) twice, k2 tog; rep from * twice more, k1.

6th row   K3, (p1, k2) twice, p1, k1, (p2 tog, p1) 3 times, p2 tog, p2, p1, k2.

7th row   Sl1, k2 tog, (yrn) twice, k2 tog, yrn, sl1, k2 tog, psso, k1, sl1, k2 tog, psso, k11.

8th row   Cast off 6 sts loosely (1 st now on right-hand needle), k4, p3 tog, k3, p1, k2).

These 8 rows form the pattern. Repeat them until the strip is the required length.

14　Pram or cot cover

44　Leaf pattern pram or cot cover, pattern 14

Generations of babies have been treated to coverlets similar to this one. The four decorative raised leaves tend to make the casual viewer assume that all the patterns are alike but closer inspection will usually reveal small differences. Before patterns were printed they were passed on by knitters who simply copied them or the directions were handed on by word of mouth. It is easy to see how small alterations occurred, albeit unintentionally.

This particular example is worked in an angora-look yarn. The yarn is very soft, and although the borders here have been hand-knitted, the edges could be covered in satin ribbon.

Materials
19 balls (20 g) Twilley Bobtail, angora-look
Pair 3¾ mm knitting needles

Measurements
83 cm (33 in) wide; 105 cm (43 in) long, including borders

Tension
Each square measures 12.5 cm (5 in) along each side.

Abbreviation
M1   make 1 st by working yrn.

To make
The square   Make 48 pieces.
Cast on 2 sts.
1st row   K1, m1, k1.
2nd row and foll alt rows to 6th row   P.
3rd row   (K1, m1) twice, k1.
5th row   (K1, m1) 4 times, k1.
7th row   K1, m1, p1, k2, m1, k1, m1, k2, p1, m1, k1.
8th row   P2, k1, p7, k1, p2.
9th row   K1, m1, p2, k3, m1, k1, m1, k3, p2, m1, k1.
10th row   P2, k2, p9, k2, p2.
11th row   K1, m1, p3, k4, m1, k1, m1, k4, p3, m1, k1.
12th row   P2, k3, p11, k3, p2.
13th row   K1, m1, p4, k5, m1, k1, m1, k5, p4, m1, k1.
14th row   P2, k4, p13, k4, p2.
15th row   K1, m1, p5, k6, m1, k1, m1, k6, p5, m1, k1.
16th row   P2, k5, p15, k5, p2.
17th row   K1, m1, p6, sl1, k1, psso, k11, k2 tog, p6, m1, k1.
18th row   P2, k6, p13, k6, p2.
19th row   K1, m1, p to centre leaf panel, sl1, k1, psso, k to last 2 sts of leaf panel, k2 tog, p to last st, m1, k1.
20th row   P the k and m sts and k the p sts of the previous row.
Repeat the last 2 rows 4 times.
29th row   K1, m1, p12, sl1, k2 tog, psso, p12, m1, k1.
30th row   P to end.
31st row   K to end inc 1 st at both end of the row (*31 sts*).
32nd and 33rd rows   As 30th row.
34th row   K2 tog, *m1, k2 tog; rep from * to last 3 sts, m1, k3 tog.
35th row   P to end.
36th row   P to end, dec 1 st at both ends of row.
37th row   K to end.
38th row   As 36th row.
39th row   P to end.
Repeat 34th to 39th rows 3 times, then 34th to 37th rows once only.
Purl remaining 3 sts together and fasten off.

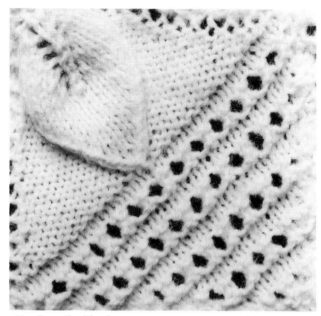

45   *Detail of leaf pattern square, pattern 14*

To make up

Placing the leaf points together, join four sections into a larger square. When all twelve large squares have been completed, join these together in four strips of three large squares. Mattress seam, with the right side of the work facing, is the most suitable for sewing these squares together.

The border

With right side of work facing, using $3\frac{3}{4}$ mm needles, pick up and knit 171 sts evenly along the length of the side edge. Work 1 row moss stitch, then continue in moss stitch, *at the same time* increasing 1 st at both ends of every row, until border measures 4 cm ($1\frac{1}{2}$ in). Cast off. Work the remaining long border in the same way.

The width borders are worked in the same way, but picking up and knitting 129 sts only, before working and increasing for the border.

With right side of work facing, mitre the corners by sewing together with a flat seam, taking just the edge stitch from each side and drawing these together very gently to avoid a bulky seam.

15 Lace curtains or screen

46 *Knitted lacy curtains, pattern 15*

Creating handmade curtains from your own handworked fabric could be considered quite a challenge; however, when the cloth is assembled from strips of knitting the possibilities are fascinating and the task is altogether easier.

This example is made with an insertion pattern through the centre, with the same pattern having an added point border for the outer strips. The curtains here are intended for small cottage-type windows, but by adding more insertion strips before sewing on those with borders the curtains can be any width you require, and, of course, they may be knitted to any length.

To use this idea as a screen, add at least 5 cm (2 in) to the top and bottom, so that the ends can be sewn into a channel for a piece of dowelling to be inserted. Curtains could also be hung onto dowelling rod at the top, or, if preferred, separate loops could be worked for the rod to pass through.

Materials
7 balls (50 g) Twilley Stalite No 3 cotton
Pair 5 mm knitting needles

Measurements
The quantities listed above will provide two curtains, each 56 cm (22 in) wide, 86 cm (34 in) long.

Tension
Each pattern repeat measures 15 cm (6 in) wide and 8.5 cm (3½ in) deep.

To make the border strips Make four pieces alike.
With 5 mm needles, cast on 33 sts loosely.
1st row K1, yrn, p2 tog, *k11, k2 tog, yrn twice to make 2 sts, k2 tog, k10* yrn, p2 tog, k1, yfwd, k2.
2nd row K4, yrn, p2 tog, *k12, p1 in second made st of 1st row, k12* yrn, p2 tog, k1.
3rd row K1, yrn, p2 tog, *k9, (k2 tog, yrn twice to make 2 sts, k2 tog) twice, k8, *yrn, p2 tog, k2, yfwd, k2.
4th row K5, yrn, p2 tog, *k10, p1 in second made st of previous row, k3, p1, k10, *yrn, p2 tog, k1.
5th row K1, yrn, p2 tog, *k7, (k2 tog, yrn twice to make 2 sts, k2 tog) 3 times, k6, *yrn, p2 tog, k3, yfwd, k2.
6th row K6, yrn, p2 tog, *k8, (p1 in second made st of previous row, k3) twice, p1 in second made st of previous row, k8, *yrn, p2 tog, k1.
7th row K1, yrn, p2 tog, *k5, (k2 tog, yrn twice to make 2 sts, k2 tog) 4 times, k4, *yrn, p2 tog, k2 tog, yrn twice to make 2 sts, k2, yfwd, k2.
8th row K6, p1 in second made st of previous row, k1, yrn, p2 tog, *k6, p1 in second made st of previous row, (k3, p1 in second made st of previous row) 3 times, k6, *yrn, p2 tog, k1.
9th row K1, yrn, p2 tog, *k3, (k2 tog, yrn twice to make 2 sts, k2 tog) 5 times, k2, *yrn, p2 tog, k8.

47 *Curtain strip with lace border, pattern 15*

10th row   Cast off 5 sts loosely (1 st now on right-hand needle), k2, yrn, p2 tog, *k4, p1 in second made st of previous row, (k3, p1 in second made st of previous row) 4 times, k4, *yrn, p2 tog, k1.

11th row   K1, yrn, p2 tog, *k5, (k2 tog, yrn twice to make 2 sts, k2 tog) 4 times, k4, *yrn, p2 tog, k1, yfwd, k2.

12th row   K4, yrn, p2 tog, *k6, p1, (k3, p1) 3 times, k6, *yrn, p2 tog, k1.

13th row   K1, yrn, p2 tog, *k7, (k2 tog, yrn twice to make 2 sts, k2 tog) 3 times, k6, *yrn, p2 tog, k2, yfwd, k2.

14th row   K5, yrn, p2 tog, *k8, p1, (k3, p1) twice, k8, *yrn, p2 tog, k1.

15th row   K1, yrn, p2 tog, *k9, (k2 tog, yrn twice to make 2 sts, k2 tog) twice, k8, *yrn, p2 tog, k3, yfwd, k2.

16th row   K6, yrn, p2 tog, *k10, p1, k3, p1, k10, *yrn, p2 tog, k1.

17th row   K1, yrn, p2 tog, *k11, k2 tog, yrn twice to make 2 sts, k2 tog, k10, *yrn, p2 tog, k2 tog, yrn twice to make 2 sts, k2, yfwd, k2.

18th row   K6, p1, k1, yrn, p2 tog, *k12, p1, k12, *yrn, p2 tog, k1.

19th row   K1, yrn, p2 tog, *k2, k2 tog, yrn twice to make 2 sts, k2 tog, k13, k2 tog, yrn twice to make 2 sts, k2 tog, k2, *yrn, p2 tog, k8.

20th row   Cast off 5 sts loosely (1 st now on right-hand needle), k2, yrn, p2 tog, *k4, p1 in second made st of previous row, k16, p1 in second made st of previous row, k3, *yrn, p2 tog, k1.

These 20 rows form the pattern including the outer borders. Repeat them until the curtains are 56 cm (22 in) long, ending after nearest 20th pattern row. Cast off loosely.

To make the insertion strips   Make two pieces.

These are simply the strips as given above without the borders. Cast on 25 sts and work in pattern as above, working only the pattern as it forms between * and * on every row.

Continue with the pattern until the strip is exactly the same number of rows as the outer pieces. Cast off.

To make up

With right side facing, join the strips with a flat seam so that, when hanging, the curtains appear to be in one continuous width.

To make hanging loops, cast on 9 sts. Cast off. Join these tiny cords into a circle and sew them at intervals to top of curtain. These loops will serve for narrow dowelling. Should larger-diameter rods be used, cast on more stitches (do not knit the stitches but cast them off immediately).

If the curtains are to be used as a screen, allow a little more yarn and work an extra 10 cm (4 in) before casting off. Fold the extra fabric to the wrong side of the work and slip stitch hem in place.

16 Leaf pattern cushion cover

48 *Leaf pattern knitted cushion cover, pattern 16*

Any of the square patterned bedspreads will lend themselves to being
adapted for cushion covers. The motif for pattern 3 has been chosen for
this cover and it has a plain stocking-stitch back. Using the quantities as a
guide, you could make quite a collection of these attractive cushions, to
complement the bedspread itself, or for the adornment of living-room
chairs.

The yarn used and the close knitting will give many years of hard wear.

Materials

6 hanks (100 g) Twilley Handicraft No 1 cotton
Pair 3¾ mm knitting needles
40 cm (16 in) zip fastener

Measurements

46 cm (18 in) along each side edge

Tension

22 sts and 30 rows to 10 cm (4 in) measured over stocking stitch

To make

For the front of this cover, make four squares following the pattern
instructions for the leaf bedspread pattern 3, page 34.

The back

With 3¾ mm needles, cast on 100 sts.
Beginning with a knit row, continue in stocking stitch until work measures
46 cm (18 in), ending after a purl row. Cast off.

To make up

Join the four squares into one large square with the leaves to the centre as
on the bedspread. Place the right side of this square to the knit side of the
stocking-stitch back and seam with back stitch round three of the sides and
2.5 cm (1 in) into the fourth side. Turn the cover to the right side and
insert the zip fastener.

The crochet patterns

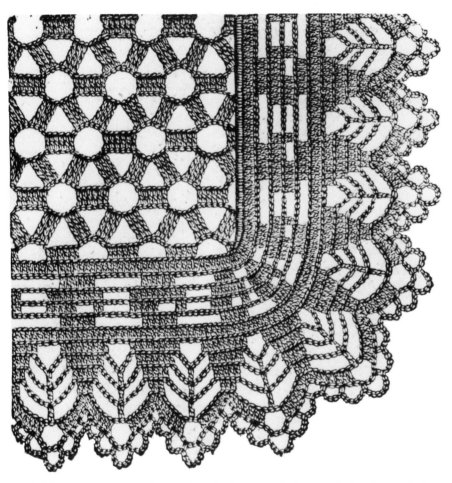

In fashion garments crochet, unlike knitting, only has periods of popularity, but for household articles it has permanent pride of place. As a craft it has many advantages. At its finest it imitates beautiful lace, at its thickest it can be used for floor rugs, and between these two extremes can be found a huge assortment of stitch patterns which, for the most part, lie wonderfully flat. Added to this is the bonus that, once acquired, the skill of crochet is tremendously fast.

Many of the items shown in this section have a traditional background. None of them is particularly grand in conception, so any one item is as suitable for the novice to work as the experienced worker. Wherever possible they have been revived in the piece-by-piece method, so that the small sections may be easily carried about.

1 Fine lace bedspread

The squares of this bedspread are relatively simple to work. However, the beginner to crochet may find the yarn very fine to use. It is suggested that the square is practised in a thicker yarn before beginning the fine squares. The more experienced craftswoman will find no problem and this bedspread has one great advantage: the squares are joined in the working.

The quantity of yarn suggested covers the making of the squares only; should you decide to add a fringe, add a few extra balls for this purpose. Unfringed, the lace makes a delicate window screen or a handsome tablecloth for special occasions (see page 51).

Materials
36 balls (20 g) Twilley Twenty Crochet Cotton No 20
1.5 mm crochet hook

Measurements
Width, 169 cm (68¾ in); length, 221 cm (89¼ in)

Tension
Each small square measures 13 cm (5¼ in) along each side.

To make
First motif
Make 8 ch and join into a ring with sl st.
1st round   Work 16 dc into ring and join with sl st to 1st dc.
2nd round   1 dc in same st, *7 ch, miss 3 dc, 1 dc in next dc; rep from * twice, 7 ch, sl st in 1st dc.
3rd round   *(1 dc, 1 htr, 2 tr, 3 dtr, 2 tr, 1 htr, 1 dc) all in next 7-ch sp; rep from * 3 times, sl st in 1st dc.
4th round   Sl st to centre dtr, 1 dc in same st, *7 ch, miss 2 sts, (leaving last loop of each st on hook work 1 tr in next st, miss 4 sts, 1 tr in next st, yrh and draw through all 3 loops) – cluster worked – 7 ch, miss 2 sts, 1 dc in centre dtr; rep from * 3 times, omitting 1 dc at end of last rep, sl st in 1st dc.
5th round   3 ch, (1 tr, 3 ch, 2 tr) in same st, *3 ch, 3 tr in next 7-ch sp, 1 tr in cluster, 3 tr in next 7-ch sp, 3 ch, (2 tr, 3 ch, 2 tr) in next dc; rep from * 3 times, omitting the (2 tr, 3 ch, 2 tr) group at end of last rep, sl st to top of 3 ch.
6th round   Sl st to 3-ch sp, (3 ch, 1 tr, 3 ch, 2 tr) in same sp, *5 ch, miss next sp and next tr, 1 tr in each of next 5 tr, 5 ch, miss next sp, (2 tr, 3 ch, 2 tr) in next 3-ch sp; rep from * 3 times, omitting (2 tr, 3 ch, 2 tr) group at end of last rep, sl st to top of 3 ch.
7th round   Sl st to 3-ch sp, 3 ch, (2 tr, 3 ch, 3 tr) in same sp, *7 ch, miss

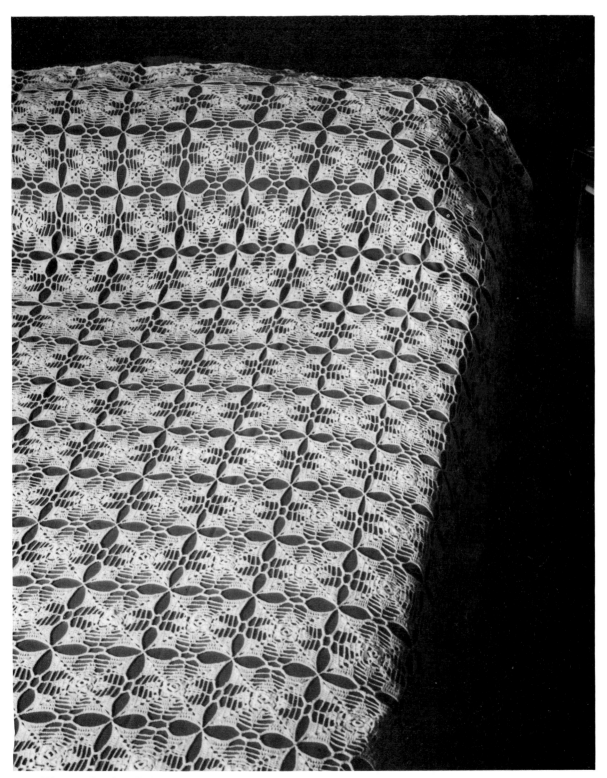

49   *Fine crochet lace bedspread, pattern 1*

next sp and next tr, 1 tr in each of next 3 tr, 7 ch, (3 tr, 3 ch, 3 tr) in next 3-ch sp; rep from * 3 times, omitting (3 tr, 3 ch, 3 tr) at end of last rep, sl st to top of 3 ch.

8th round 3 ch, *1 tr in each of next 2 tr, (3 tr, 3 ch, 3 tr) in 3-ch sp, 1 tr in each of next 3 tr, 9 ch, miss 1 tr, 1 tr in next tr, 9 ch, 1 tr in next tr; rep from * 3 times, omitting 1 tr at end of last rep, sl st to top of 3 ch.

9th round 3 ch, *1 tr in each of next 5 sts, (3 dtr, 5 ch, 3 dtr) in 3-ch sp, 1 tr in each of next 6 tr, 9 ch, 1 tr in next tr, 9 ch, 1 tr in next tr; rep from * 3 times, omitting 1 tr at end of last rep, sl st to top of 3 ch.

10th round 1 dc in same st, *1 dc in each of next 8 sts, 3 dc in 5-ch sp, 5 ch, sl st in last dc – corner picot worked – 2 dc in same ch sp, 1 dc in each of next 9 sts, (6 dc in next 9-ch sp, 3 ch, sl st in last dc – side picot worked – 5 dc in same ch-sp) twice, 1 dc in next tr; rep from * 3 times, omitting 1 dc at end of last rep, sl st to 1st dc. Fasten off.

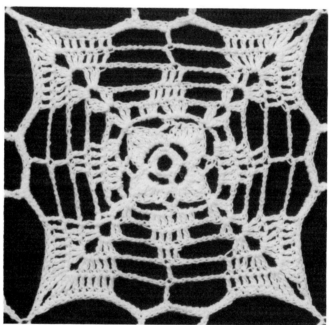

50 *Square of crochet lace, pattern 1*

Second motif

Work as first motif to the end of the 9th round.

10th (joining) round 1 dc in same st, *1 dc in each of next 8 sts, 3 dc in 5-ch sp, 2 ch, sl st to corner picot of first motif, 2 ch, sl st in last dc on second motif, 2 dc in same ch sp, 1 dc in each of next 9 sts, *(6 dc in 9-ch sp, 1 ch, sl st in side picot of first motif, 1 ch, sl st in last dc of second motif, 5 dc in same ch sp) twice, 1 dc in next st; rep from * to * once, (6 dc, 1 side picot, 5 dc) in same ch sp; rep the bracketed section of 10th round of first motif once, 1 dc in next tr; rep from * of 10th round of first motif twice, omitting 1 dc at end of last rep, sl st to 1st dc. Fasten off. Continue in this way until a strip of 13 squares has been completed. Join next motif to side of first motif then continue joining motifs to previous motif and to side of previous motif strip until 17 strips have been completed.

To complete

If a fringe is required, cut supply of yarn into 25 cm (10 in) lengths. Using six strands together, fold in half, using hook, draw the doubled loops through, wrap ends round hook and draw through the loops; pull to secure. Repeat this action at intervals along the side edges.

The same motif can be used to make a tablecloth. Decide on the finished size of the tablecloth and from this estimate the number of motifs required (see page 9).

51 Fine crochet lace bedspread in use as a tablecloth, pattern 1

2 Fan swirl bedspread

52 *Crochet lace swirl strip bedspread, pattern 2*

The name given to this pattern derives from the fan shape which alternates from side to side of the strips. It is easily and rapidly worked and as it is made in sections it is readily transportable. The yarn used for this example is quite thick, producing a richly-textured quilt – a finer yarn will give a lace effect; it is worth experimenting with different yarns to see which fabric best suits your requirements.

This particular design when worked in suitable yarn will also make a beautiful christening shawl for a baby. Similarly, made in shorter strips it can be adapted for use as a pram or cot cover.

Materials
33 hanks (100 g) Twilley Handicraft No 1 cotton
4 mm crochet hook

Measurements
Width, 204 cm (81 in); length, 228 cm (90 in)

Tension
To obtain these measurements each strip should measure 17 cm ($6\frac{3}{4}$ in) wide.

To make
First strip
Make 28 ch.

1st row   1 dc in 8th ch from hook, 3 ch, miss 3 ch, 1 dc in next ch, turn.

2nd row   3 ch, 4 tr in next sp, 1 tr in next dc, 4 tr in next sp, turn.

3rd row   4 ch, 1 tr in next tr, (2 ch, miss 1 tr, 1 tr in next tr) 4 times, 2 ch, 1 tr in last dc of first row, miss 2 base ch, sl st in next base ch st, 1 ch, miss 1 base ch st, sl st in next base ch st, turn.

4th row   (1 tr in next tr, 2 tr in next sp) 5 times, 1 tr in next tr, 1 tr in last sp, 1 tr in 3rd ch, turn.

5th row   3 ch, (1 tr in next tr, 1 ch, miss 1 tr) 5 times, (1 tr in next tr, 2 ch, miss 1 tr) 3 times, 1 tr in next tr, miss 2 base ch sts, sl st in next base ch st, turn.

6th row   3 ch, (miss next sp, 1 dc in next tr, 3 ch) twice, miss next sp, 1 dc in next tr, turn.

7th row   Miss next sp, 1 tr in next dc, 2 tr in next sp, 1 tr in next dc, 3 tr in next sp, miss 1 base ch st, sl st in next base ch st, 2 ch, miss 1 base ch st, sl st in next base ch st, turn.

8th row   2 ch, miss next tr (1 tr in next tr, 2 ch) 6 times, sl st in next sp on previous motif, turn.

9th row   (2 tr in next sp, 1 tr in next tr) 6 times, 2 tr in next sp, 1 tr in sl st, miss 1 base ch st, sl st in next base ch st, 2 ch, miss 1 base ch st, sl st in last base ch st, turn.

10th row   2 ch, (miss 1 tr, 1 tr in next tr, 3 ch) 3 times, (miss 1 tr, 1 tr in next tr, 2 ch) 7 times, miss 1 tr, 1 tr in next st, sl st in next sp on previous motif, turn.

11th row   3 ch, (miss next sp, 1 dc in next tr, 3 ch) twice, miss next sp, 1 dc in next tr, turn.

12th row   Miss next sp, 1 tr in next dc, 2 tr in next sp, 1 tr in next dc, 3 tr in next sp, sl st in sp on previous motif, 1 ch, sl st in next sp on previous motif, turn.

13th row   2 ch, miss next tr, (1 tr in next tr, 2 ch) 6 times, sl st in next sp on previous motif, 1 ch, sl st in next tr on previous motif, turn.

14th row   (2 tr in next sp, 1 tr in next tr) 6 times, 2 tr in next sp, 1 tr in next st, sl st in next sp on previous motif, 1 ch, sl st in last sp on previous motif, turn.

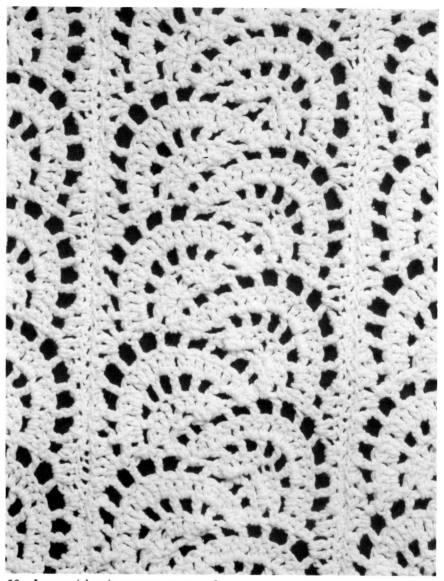

53   Lace swirl strip pattern, pattern 2

15th row   2 ch, (miss 1 tr, 1 tr in next tr, 3 ch) 3 times, (miss 1 tr, 1 tr in next tr, 2 ch) 7 times, miss 1 tr, 1 tr in next st, sl st in next sp on previous motif, turn.

16th row   3 ch, (miss next sp, 1 dc in next tr, 3 ch) twice, miss next sp, 1 dc in next tr, turn.

17th row   Miss next sp, 1 tr in next dc, 2 tr in next sp, 1 tr in next dc, 3 tr in next sp, sl st in next tr on previous motif, 1 ch, sl st in next sp on previous motif, turn.

18th row   2 ch, miss next tr, (1 tr in next tr, 2 ch) 6 times, sl st in next sp on previous motif, 1 ch, sl st in next sp on previous motif, turn.

19th row (2 tr in next sp, 1 tr in next tr) 6 times, 2 tr in next sp, 1 tr in next st, sl st in next tr on previous motif, 1 ch, sl st in next sp on previous motif, turn.

Repeat 15th to 19th rows for pattern until strip measures approx 228 cm (90 in) ending after nearest 15th row.

Continue along 15th row thus: (4 tr in next sp) 3 times, 3 ch, turn.

Next row 3 ch, (miss 1 tr, 1 tr in next tr, 1 ch) 6 times, sl st in 1st sp on previous motif. Fasten off.

Make 11 more strips in the same way.

To complete

With right side facing, join in yarn at one corner and work a row of double crochet along all edges, working in treble between motifs to straighten the edges. Fasten off.

The strips may be sewn together, but a crochet join is faster and neater. Place two strips together, right sides facing, insert hook through back loop only of each edge stitch, draw loop through, yarn round hook and through all loops on hook. Continue in this way to end of strip.

The border

A narrow border was added to complement the strip pattern and this was worked directly on to the fabric. There are many suitable borders that may be worked and sewn to the edges but care should be taken to avoid very wide borders since these might detract from the main pattern.

To make

Join yarn in corner st, 4 ch, (1 tr, 1 ch) twice in same st, 1 tr in same st, *miss 3 sts, 1 tr in next st, (1 ch, 1 tr) 3 times in same st; rep from * to end, sl st in 3rd of 4 ch. Fasten off.

3 Octagon and square bedspread

The motifs that form this bedspread are joined in such a way as to leave natural breaks in the fabric, giving an opportunity to show off your favourite throwover quilt or a new fabric shade that will set it off and tie in with the general colour scheme.

While this design is not recommended for use as a tablecloth, the octagon motifs would serve very well as place mats, and the basic pattern can be repeated to form a large centre mat.

54　Crochet octagon and square bedspread, pattern 3

Materials
34 balls (50 g) Twilley Stalite No 3 cotton
3.5 mm crochet hook

Measurements
Width 162 cm (64 in); length 204 cm (80 in)

Tension
To obtain these measurements the octagon motifs should have a diameter
of 20 cm (8 in) and the filler square motifs should be 6 cm (2½ in) square.

Special abbreviation
Dtrf   double treble front worked thus: bring hook to front of work and
inserting hook from right to left work a double treble round the stem of the
next treble.

To make
Octagon motif   Make a total of 60 pieces.
Make 5 ch and join into a ring with sl st into first ch.

1st round   5 ch, (1 tr in ring, 2 ch), 7 times, sl st in 3rd of 5 ch. Do not
turn.

2nd round   Sl st in 2-ch sp, 3 ch, 4 tr in same sp, 1 ch, (5 tr in next sp,
1 ch) 7 times, sl st in 3rd ch.

3rd round   3 ch, (2 tr in next tr, work dtrf round next tr, 2 tr in next tr,
1 tr in next tr, 1 ch, 1 tr in next tr) 8 times, omitting 1 tr in next tr at end
of last rep, sl st in 3rd ch.

4th round   3 ch, (1 tr in each of next 2 tr, 1 dtrf round next st, 1 tr in each
of next 3 tr, 2 ch, 1 tr in next tr) 8 times, omitting 1 tr in next tr at end of
last rep, sl st in top of 3 ch.

5th and 6th rounds   3 ch, (1 tr in each of next 2 tr, 1 dtrf round dtrf, 1 tr in
each of next 3 tr, 3 ch, 1 tr in next tr) 8 times, omitting 1 tr in next tr at
end of last rep, sl st in top of 3 ch.

7th round   3 ch, (1 tr in next tr, 2 tr in next tr, 1 dtrf round dtrf, 2 tr in
next tr, 1 tr in each of next 2 tr, 3 ch, 1 tr in next tr) 8 times, omitting 1 tr
in next tr at end of last rep, sl st in top of 3 ch.

8th round   3 ch, (1 tr in each of next 2 tr, 2 tr in next tr, 1 dtrf round dtrf,
2 tr in next tr, 1 tr in each of next 3 tr, 3 ch, 1 tr in next tr) 8 times,
omitting 1 tr in next tr at end of last rep, sl st in top of 3 ch.

9th round   1 ch, 1 dc in top of 3 ch, (1 htr in each of next 2 tr, 1 tr in next
tr, 1 dtr in next tr, 1 dtrf round dtrf, 1 dtr in next tr, 1 tr in next tr, 1 htr,
in each of next 2 tr, 1 dc in next tr, 1 sl st in each of next 3 ch, 1 dc in next
tr) 8 times, omitting 1 dc in next tr at end of last rep, sl st in first ch.
Fasten off.

When working remaining octagon motifs, work to the end of the 8th round
and join thus:

9th round   1 dc in same st as sl st, 1 htr in each of next 2 tr, 1 tr in next tr,
1 dtr in next tr, 1 dtrf round next dtrf, sl st to top of dtrf of first motif, 1

55 *Octagon and square motifs, pattern 3*

dtr in tr on second motif, 1 tr in next tr, 1 htr in each of next 2 tr, 1 dc in next tr, 1 sl st in each of next 3 ch, 1 dc in next tr, 1 htr in each of next 2 tr, 1 tr in next tr, 1 dtrf round next dtrf, sl st to top of adjacent dtrf of first motif, then complete as remainder of 9th round of first motif. Continue in this way working remaining octagon motifs, joining as last motif was joined to the first motif, attaching on one, two or three sides as required to form 8 motifs across the width and 10 motifs along the length.

Filler motifs

Make 5 ch and join into a ring with sl st into first ch.

1st round 3 ch (stands as 1st tr), 3 tr into ring, (1 ch, 4 tr into ring) 3 times, 1 ch, join with sl st to top of 3 ch.

2nd round Sl st along to first 1-ch sp, 3 ch (stands as 1st tr), (2 tr, 2 ch, 3 tr) all in 1-ch sp, (3 tr, 2 ch, 3 tr, all in next 1-ch sp) 3 times, join with sl st to top of 3 ch.

3rd round Sl st along to next 2-ch sp, 3 ch, 2 tr, 1 ch, sl st in centre of 3 sl sts between two points of one octagon motif, 1 ch, 3 tr in same 2-ch sp, (3 tr between next two sets of 3 tr along one side, 3 tr, 1 ch, sl st in centre of 3 sl sts of adjacent octagon motif, 1 ch, 3 tr in next 2-ch sp) 3 times, 3 tr between next two sets of 3 tr along last side, join with sl st to top of 3 ch. Fasten off.

To complete

The bedspread may be embellished with tassels to make the outer edges of the octagons hang well, or the crochet may be lined with contrasting cloth.

4   Irish crochet granny squares bedspread

A truly old-fashioned 'patchwork' bedcover. The squares are frequently worked in colours, but the raised texture of the traditional stitch patterns gives lustre to the natural quality of pure cotton, and it looks exactly right in white.

The spread takes quite a large number of squares but they are very quickly made – why not work with a friend and enjoy watching the pile of squares grow?

Materials

33 hanks (100 g) Twilley Handicraft No 1 cotton
4 mm crochet hook

Measurements

Width, 167 cm (66 in); length, 228 cm (90 in) excluding border.

Tension

Each square should measure 15 cm (6 in) along each side to obtain the measurements stated above.

56 *Irish crochet granny squares bedspread, pattern 4*

1 Canterbury bell knitted bedspread. *Pattern 1*

2 Octagon pattern knitted bedspread. *Pattern 5*

3 Machine knitted bedspread. *Pattern 8*

4   Lace and moss pattern knitted tablecloth. *Pattern 9*

5   Lace swirl knitted table linen. *Pattern 10*

6 Knitted pleated tea cosy. *Pattern 11*

7 Leaf pattern knitted cushion cover. *Pattern 16*

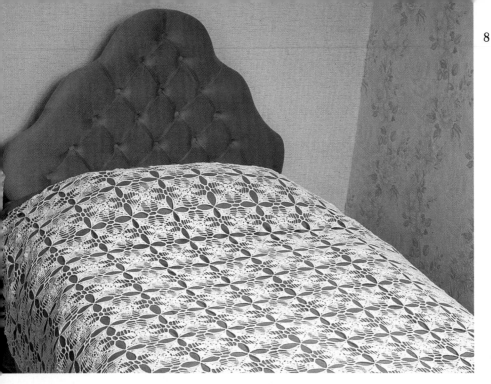

8 Fine lace crochet bedspread. *Pattern 1*

9 Fine lace crochet used as tablecloth. *Pattern 1*

10   Octagon and square crochet bedspread. *Pattern 3*

11 Crochet table linen. *Pattern 7*

12 Crochet tray cloth, full size. *Pattern 8*

57   Irish crochet popcorn motif, pattern 4

Popcorn motif   Make 83 pieces.

Make 4 ch, join into ring with sl st.

1st round   3 ch, 11 tr into ring, join with sl st in top of 3 ch.

2nd round   3 ch, 5 tr between 3 ch and 1 tr on first round, (miss 3 tr, 6 tr
between trs) 3 times, miss 3 tr, sl st in top of 3 ch.

3rd round   3 ch, 2 tr at base of 3 ch, (miss 3 tr, 6 tr between trs, miss 3 tr,
3 tr between trs) 3 times, miss 3 tr, 6 tr between trs, sl st in top of 3 ch.

4th round   3 ch, 2 tr between last and first groups at base of 3 ch, (miss 3
tr, 3 tr between trs, miss 3 tr, 6 tr between trs, miss 3 tr, 3 tr between trs) 3
times, miss 3 tr, 6 tr between trs, sl st in top of 3 ch.

5th round   3 ch, 4 tr between last and first groups at base of 3 ch, remove
hook, insert hook into top of 3 ch, then into dropped loop and draw loop
through, 3 ch, miss 3 tr, *(5 tr between trs, remove hook, insert hook into
first of 5 tr, then into dropped loop and draw loop through – a popcorn
made – 3 ch, miss 3 tr) twice, (1 popcorn, 3 ch, 1 popcorn) between trs,
3 ch, miss 3 tr, 1 popcorn between trs, 3 ch, miss 3 tr; rep from * twice
more, (1 popcorn between trs, 3 ch, miss 3 tr) twice, (1 popcorn, 3 ch,
1 popcorn) between trs, 3 ch, miss 3 tr, sl st in top of 3 ch.

6th round   3 ch, 2 tr in previous 3-ch sp, *(3 tr in next 3-ch sp) 3 times, 6 tr in next sp, 3 tr in next sp; rep from * twice more, (3 tr in next sp) 3 times, 6 tr in next sp, sl st in top of 3 ch. Fasten off.

58   *Irish crochet rose motif, pattern 4*

Rose motif   Make 82 pieces.

Make 4 ch and join into ring with sl st.

1st round   *2 ch, 4 tr into ring, sl st into ring; rep from * 3 times more.

2nd round   Sl st in back of 3rd tr, *keeping yarn in back of work, 4 ch, sl st in 3rd tr of next group; rep from * twice more, 4 ch, join with sl st to first sl st.

3rd round   Into each 4-ch loop work 1 sl st, 5 tr, 1 sl st, making four petals.

4th round   *6 ch, 1 sl st into back of sl st between petals; rep from * 3 times more.

5th round   3 ch, (2 tr, 3 ch, 3 tr) into same 6-ch loop, *1 ch, (3 tr, 3 ch, 3 tr) into next loop; rep from * twice more, 1 ch, join with sl st to 3rd of 3 ch.

6th round   3 ch, (2 tr, 3 ch, 3 tr) into same sp, *1 ch, 3 tr into 1-ch sp, 1

94

ch, (3 tr, 3 ch, 3 tr) into 3-ch sp; rep from * twice more, 1 ch, 3 tr into 1-ch
sp, 1 ch, join with sl st to 3rd of 3 ch.

7th round   3 ch, (2 tr, 3 ch, 3 tr) into same sp, *(1 ch, 3 tr into 1-ch sp)
twice, 1 ch, (3 tr, 3 ch, 3 tr) into 3-ch sp; rep from * twice more, (1 ch, 3 tr
into 1-ch sp) twice, 1 ch, join with sl st to 3rd of 3 ch.

Work 2 more rounds in this way, repeating the sections in brackets
(parentheses) 3 times more instead of twice. Fasten off.

To make up

Join the squares alternately, with 11 squares to the width and 15 squares to
the length, noting that there will be a popcorn motif in each corner. This
example was joined four squares at a time for ease of work, with right sides
facing, and sewn through the back loops of the last rows. This method
leaves a neat edging on the right side of the work.

5   Border for Irish crochet bedspread

59   Border for Irish crochet bedspread, pattern 5

The quantities given for the bedspread will be sufficient to make this
narrow border, and the same size of crochet hook as that used for the
squares will produce a suitable tension.

Join yarn in one corner of the completed bedspread.

1st round   *5 ch, miss 3 sts, 1 dc into next space between trs; rep from * all round outer edge, working an uneven number of dc to each side and turning the corners with 5 ch. Join to first st with sl st.

2nd round   3 ch (stands as 1st tr), 2 tr, 3 ch, 3 tr in next 5-ch loop, *1 dc in next 5-ch loop, 3 tr, 3 ch, 3 tr in next 5-ch loop; rep from * to end, working 1 dc in last loop. Join to 3rd of 3 ch with sl st. Fasten off.

6   Openwork tablecloth

This will add a touch of luxury for afternoon tea or provide a centre-piece at a dinner party if it is laid over a large cloth of a contrasting colour. Although it is made in one piece, this cloth is not heavy to work or to carry about in the making because a lightweight yarn is used to produce this lacy pattern.

The fabric hangs well, making it suitable for use as a window screen (see page 00). For really dedicated crochet workers there might also be the prospect of a bedspread in this design, simply adding on 18 ch for each extra repeat of the pattern for the added width. The amount of extra yarn required for a bedspread may be calculated from the quantities given for this size of tablecloth (see page 00).

Materials
13 balls (25 g) Twilley Lyscordet No 5 cotton
2 mm crochet hook

Measurements
91 cm (36 in) along each side edge, excluding border

Tension
Each repeat of pattern measures 8 cm (3 in) in width.

To make
Make 221 ch.

1st row   1 tr in 4th ch from hook, 1 tr in next ch, *(5 ch, miss 3 ch, 1 dc in next ch) 3 times, 5 ch, miss 3 ch, 1 tr in each of next 3 ch; rep from *11 times more, 5 ch, turn.

2nd row   *3 tr in next loop, (5 ch, 1 dc in next loop) twice, 5 ch, 3 tr in next loop, 2 ch; rep from * to end, ending 1 tr in 3rd of turning ch, 5 ch, turn.

3rd row   *1 tr in each of next 3 tr, 3 tr in next loop, 5 ch, 1 dc in next

60 *Openwork crochet tablecloth, pattern 6*

loop, 5 ch, 3 tr in next loop, 1 tr in each of next 3 tr, 2 ch; rep from * to end, ending 1 tr in 3rd of 5 ch, 5 ch, turn.

4th row   *1 tr in each of next 6 tr, 3 tr in next loop, 2 ch, 3 tr in next loop, 1 tr in each of next 6 tr, 2 ch; rep from * to end, ending 1 tr on 3rd of 5 ch, 1 ch, turn.

5th row   *1 dc in next sp, 5 ch, miss 3 tr, 1 tr in each of next 6 tr, 2 ch, 1 tr in each of next 6 tr, 5 ch; rep from * to end, ending 1 dc in last sp, 5 ch, turn.

6th row   1 dc in next loop, *5 ch, miss 3 tr, 1 tr in each of next 3 tr, 2 ch, 1 tr in each of 3 tr, (5 ch, 1 dc in next loop) twice; rep from * to end, omitting 5 ch and 1 dc at end of last rep, ending 2 ch, 1 tr in last dc, 5 ch, turn.

7th row   1 dc in next 2-ch loop, 5 ch, 1 dc in next loop, *5 ch, 3 tr in next 2-ch sp, (5 ch, 1 dc in next loop) 3 times; rep from * to end, omitting 5 ch and 1 dc at end of last rep, ending 2 ch, 1 tr in 3rd of 5 ch, 1 ch, turn.

8th row   1 dc in 2-ch loop, 5 ch, 1 dc in next loop, *5 ch, 3 tr in next loop, 2 ch, 3 tr in next loop, (5 ch, 1 dc in next loop) twice; rep from * to end, ending 1 dc in same loop, 5 ch, turn.

9th row   1 dc in next loop, *5 ch, 3 tr in next loop, 1 tr in each of next 3 tr, 2 ch, 1 tr in each of next 3 tr, 3 tr in next loop, 5 ch, 1 dc in next loop; rep from * to end, ending 2 ch, 1 tr in last dc, 5 ch, turn.

10th row   *3 tr in next 5-ch loop, 1 tr in each of next 6 tr, 2 ch, 1 tr in each of next 6 tr, 3 tr in next loop, 2 ch; rep from * to end, ending 1 tr in 3rd of 5 ch, 5 ch, turn.

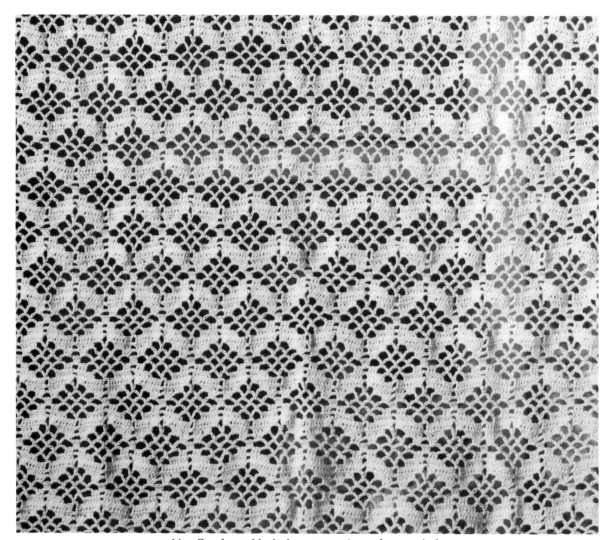

61   *Crochet tablecloth, pattern 6, used as a window screen*

11th row   *1 tr in each of next 6 tr, 5 ch, 1 dc in next sp, 5 ch, miss 3 tr,
1 tr in each of next 6 tr, 2 ch; rep from * to end, ending 1 tr in 3rd of 5 ch,
5 ch, turn.

12th row   *1 tr in each of 3 tr, (5 ch, 1 dc in next loop) twice, 5 ch, miss 3
tr, 1 tr in each of next 3 tr, 2 ch; rep from * to end, ending 1 tr in 3rd of 5
ch, 5 ch, turn.

13th row   2 tr in next sp, *(5 ch, 1 dc in next loop) 3 times, 5 ch, 3 tr in
next sp; rep from * to end, ending 5 ch, turn.

The 2nd to 13th rows form the pattern. Continue in pattern until work
measures 91 cm (36 in) ending after nearest 13th pattern row, on the *last*
13th row, work 3 ch instead of 5 ch between the 3-tr groups and omit the
5 ch at the end of the last row. Do not fasten off.

Continue with the border thus:

The border (worked in rounds)

1st round Work 1 round dc all round, outer edge, working a multiple of 4 sts. Join with sl st to first dc.

2nd round 3 ch, 1 tr in same place as sl st, 4 ch, 2 tr in same place, *3 ch, miss 3 dc, 2 tr in next dc; rep from * along side, into next corner work 2 tr, 4 ch, 2 tr. Continue in this way all round work, ending 3 ch, sl st in 3rd of 3 ch.

3rd round Sl st to next corner loop, 1 ch, into each corner loop work 4 dc, into each tr work 1 dc, into each 3-ch sp work 3 dc; join with sl st to 1st ch.

4th round Sl st to centre of corner loop, 8 ch, 1 tr in same place as last sl st, *5 ch, miss 3 dc, 1 dc in next dc; rep from * along sides, 1 tr, 5 ch, and 1 tr into centre dc of each corner, join with sl st into 3rd of 8 ch.

5th round Sl st into corner loop, 3 ch, leaving last loop on hook, make 2 tr in same loop, yrh and draw through all loops – cluster made – (5 ch, make 3-tr clusters) 4 times in same loop, *3 ch, miss next loop, 1 dc in next loop, 5 ch, 1 dc in next loop, 3 ch, miss next loop, work three 3-tr clusters with 5 ch between in next loop; rep from * along sides, into each corner loop work 5 3-tr clusters with 5 ch between, join with sl st to tip of first cluster. Fasten off.

To complete

The cloth may be pressed very lightly, preferably on a flat surface (not an ironing board). The border should be carefully blocked out with pins to retain its shape.

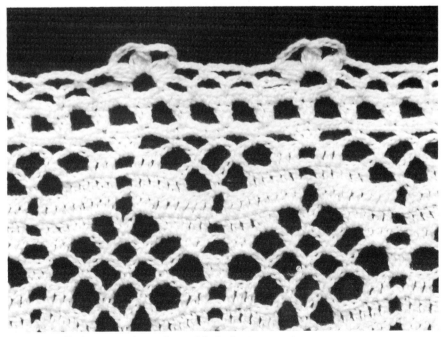

62   *Detail of openwork crochet tablecloth, pattern 6*

7   Table linen

63   *Circular crochet table linen, pattern 7*

The pattern for these place mats is repeated in the centre mat. It would also be suitable for a full-size circular tablecloth – it is simply a matter of repeating the motifs and joining them until they fit the size of cloth you wish to surround.

Materials

10 balls (25 g) Twilley Lyscordet No. 5 cotton
2 mm crochet hook
Small piece linen or cotton fabric

Measurements

Centre mat diameter 63 cm (25 in)
Place mat diameter 25 cm (10 in)
Coaster diameter 12.5 cm (5 in)

Tension

28 tr and 14 rows tr to 10 cm (4 in)

Note

1 ball cotton will make 4 coasters; 1 ball cotton will make 1 place mat; 5 balls will make the motifs for the centre mat.

The centre mat
To make first motif

Make 8 ch and join into ring with sl st.

1st round   9 ch, (1 dtr into ring, 5 ch) 7 times, join with sl st to 4th of 9 ch.

2nd round   8 dc in each 5-ch loop, sl st to first dc.

3rd round   3 ch, 1 tr in each dc to end, sl st in top of 3 ch.

4th round   4 ch, leaving last loop of each st on hook, work 1 dtr in each of next 2 tr, yrh and draw through all loops, *6 ch, miss next tr, leaving last loop on hook, work 1 dtr in each of next 3 tr, yrh and draw through all loops – 3-dtr cluster made; rep from * ending with 6 ch, sl st in top of first cluster.

5th round   8 dc in each 6-ch loop, sl st in first dc.

6th round   Sl st in next 2 dc, 3 ch, 1 tr in each of next 11 dc, *5ch, miss 4 dc, 1 tr in each of next 12 dc; rep from * ending 5 ch, sl st in top of 3 ch.

7th round   3 ch, 1 tr in each of next 11 tr, *5 ch, 1 dc in next loop, 5 ch, 1 tr in each of next 12 tr; rep from * ending 5 ch, 1 dc in next loop, 5 ch, sl st in top of 3 ch.

8th round   3 ch, 1 tr in each of next 11 tr, *(5 ch, 1 dc in next sp) twice, 5 ch, 1 tr in each of next 12 tr; rep from * ending sl st in top of 3 ch.

9th round   Sl st over next 2 tr, 3 ch, 1 tr in each of next 7 tr, *(5 ch, 1 dc in next loop) 3 times, 5 ch, miss next 2 tr, 1 tr in each of next 8 tr; rep from * ending sl st in top of 3 ch.

10th round   Sl st over next 2 tr, 3 ch, 1 tr in each of next 3 tr, *(5 ch, 1 dc in loop) 4 times, 5 ch, miss next 2 tr, 1 tr in each of next 4 tr; rep from * ending sl st in top of 3 ch. Fasten off.

To make second motif

Work as first motif to end of 9th round.

10th round   Sl st over next 2 tr, 3 ch, 1 tr in each of next 3 tr, *(5 ch, 1 dc in next loop) 4 times, 5 ch, miss next 2 tr, 1 tr in each of next 4 tr; rep from * 5 times more, 2 ch, sl st to any last worked 5-ch loop on any of the 5-ch loop sections on previous motif, (2 ch, dc in next loop on second motif, 2 ch, sl st in next loop of previous motif) 4 times, 2 ch, miss next 2 tr, 1 tr in each of next 4 tr, (5 ch, 1 dc in next loop) 4 times, 5 ch, sl st in top of 3 ch. Fasten off.

Make five more motifs, joining adjacent sides as the second motif was joined to the first motif, into a circular shape, leaving 20 loops at the outer edge and 10 loops at the centre and joining the first and last motifs to join the circle.

Border

Rejoin yarn to any 2-ch space preceding the join of motifs.

1 dc in same sp, *1 dc in corresponding 2-ch sp following join on next motif, (5 ch, 1 dc in next loop) 20 times, 5 ch, 1 dc in 2-ch sp preceding the join; rep from * ending sl st in first dc.

2nd round   7 dc in each 5-ch sp, sl st in first dc.

3rd round   Sl st over next 2 dc, 4 ch, leaving last loop on hook, work 1 dtr in each of next 2 dc, yrh and draw through all loops,* 6 ch, miss next 4 dc, work 3-dtr cluster over next 3 dc; rep from * to end, ending sl st in top of first 3-dtr cluster.

4th round   In each 6-ch sp, work 3 dc, 5 ch, sl st in first of 5 ch to form picot, 3 dc, join with sl st to first dc. Fasten off.

To complete

Lay the piece of fabric flat on a table. Place the ring of motifs on the fabric and gently move the circle until the centre is exactly equidistant between the motifs. Pin the sections in place, then neatly hem around the inner edge of the crochet to attach it to the cloth. Turn the work to the wrong side and carefully cut away the excess cloth close to the hemstitch join, leaving approximately 0.5 cm ($\frac{1}{4}$ in) rebate. Turn in this raw edge and neatly hem in place.

The place mats   Make four.
To make

Work as pattern instructions for first motif of centre mat until 10th round has been completed. Do not fasten off.

Border

1st round   Sl st to centre of next 4 tr, 5 ch, *dc in next 5-ch loop, 5 ch, rep from * to next 4 tr, 1 dc between centre of next 4 tr, 5 ch. Continue in this way all round, sl st to first sl st.

2nd round   7 dc in each 5-ch sp to end, join with sl st to first dc.

3rd round   Sl st over next 2 dc, 4 ch, 1 dtr in each of next 2 dc leaving last loop of each st on hook, yrh and draw through all loops; 6 ch, *3-dtr cluster in centre of next 7-dc group, 6 ch; rep from * to end, sl st to top of first dtr cluster.

4th round   In each 6-ch sp, work 3 dc, 5 ch, sl st in first of 5 ch, to form picot, 3 dc, join with sl st to first dc. Fasten off.

64   *Place mat of crochet table linen, pattern 7*

The coasters   Make four.

Work as pattern instructions for first motif of centre mat until the 5th round has been worked. Continue thus:
6th round   Work as previous 6th round working 2 ch, make picot, 2 ch, between each set of 12 tr instread of 5 ch. Fasten off.

To complete

Pressing is recommended for these mats. The crochet sections should be blocked (i.e. pinned out into the correct shape) and pressed lightly under a damp cloth and left to dry out completely without being disturbed. This will retain the crispness of the lace. Before pressing the centre mat make sure that the fabric used in the centre of the crochet will withstand pressing; if not, take care to avoid that area.

8   Tray cloth

65   Tray cloth of small crochet motifs, pattern 8

This neat little cloth is made from very small motifs. Having established the motif it is very tempting to add more and more to make up a useful set of household linen that will wash and wear for years. The quantities are given for the items shown, but it is easy enough to see how many squares can be made from one ball. The number of balls needed for any other article you might wish to make from this pattern can then be calculated.

Materials
3 balls (25 g) Twilley Lyscordet No 5 cotton
2 mm crochet hook

To make
First motif
Make 6 ch and join into ring with sl st.

1st round   3 ch, 1 tr into ring, (7 ch, 2 tr in ring) 3 times, 7 ch, sl st into 3rd of 3 ch.

2nd round   Sl st into next tr, sl st into next sp, 3 ch, 9 tr in same sp, (5 ch, 10 tr in next sp) 3 times, 5 ch, sl st in 3rd of 3 ch.

3rd round   3 ch, leaving last loop of each st on hook work 1 tr in each of next 4 tr, yrh and draw through all loops on hook – cluster made – *5 ch, leaving last loop of each st on hook work 1 tr in each of next 5 tr, yrh and draw through all loops on hook – 5-tr cluster made – 5 ch, in next corner loop work a 4-tr cluster, 9 ch, 4-tr cluster, 5 ch, work 5-tr cluster over next 5 tr; rep from * omitting 1 5-tr cluster at end of last rep, sl st into first cluster.

4th round   *(1 dc in each of next 3 ch, 3 ch, 1 dc in same place as last dc – picot made – 1 dc in each of next 2 ch, miss next cluster) twice, 1 dc in each of next 5 ch, 3 ch, picot, 1 dc in each of next 4 ch, miss next cluster, 1 dc in each of next 3 ch, 3 ch, picot, 1 dc in each of next 2 ch, miss next cluster; rep from * ending sl st in first dc. Fasten off.

Second motif
Work first three rounds as first motif.

4th round   (1 dc in each of next 3 ch, 3 ch, picot, 1 dc in each of next 2 ch, miss next cluster) twice, 1 dc in each of next 5 ch, 1 ch, sl st to corresponding picot of first motif, 1 ch, 1 dc in same place as last dc on (second motif, 1 dc in each of next 4 ch, miss next cluster, 1 dc in each of next 3 ch, 1 ch, sl st in corresponding picot of first motif, 1 ch, 1 dc in same place as last dc on second motif, 1 dc in each of next 2 ch, miss next cluster) 3 times, 1 dc in each of next 5 ch, 1 ch, sl st in corresponding picot on first motif, 1 ch, 1 dc in same place as last dc on second motif and complete as first motif.

To complete
Continue to make and join the motifs, working a row of six motifs for the width, and four rows of six motifs for the length to complete a cloth to the size shown. Each motif measures approx 7.5 cm ($2\frac{3}{4}$ in) square and the cloth measures approx 45 cm ($17\frac{1}{2}$ in) wide and 30 cm ($11\frac{3}{4}$ in) long. For a larger cloth it is preferable to work more motifs rather than alter the tension, which is particularly suitable for this type of pattern.

Press the work gently, using a damp cloth.

9 Armchair back and arm rests

66 *Crochet motifs used for armchair back and arm rests, pattern 9*

This pair of useful and attractive accessories is derived from the same motif as that of the tray cloth. These examples are shown to demonstrate that the possibilities for using the same pattern are endless. However, if you wish to try using squares for window screens, always consider whether the fabric will let sufficient light through and be prepared to experiment with the pattern, for example by trying a finer yarn or a looser tension to obtain a less dense effect.

Materials

6 balls (25 g) Twilley Lyscordet No 5 cotton
2 mm crochet hook
These quantities make one back and two arm rests.
9 balls make a sofa back and two arm rests

Measurements

Back rest, 45 cm (17½in) wide; 30 cm (11¾ in) deep
Arm rest, 30 cm (11¾ in) wide; 22.5 cm (8½ in) deep

To make

The single armchair back rest is made exactly as the tray cloth, crochet pattern 8. The example shown rested comfortably on the back of the chair, which was quite deep, and because of the raised nap the crochet clung well; where the back of the chair is narrow or perhaps the top is wooden or otherwise slippery, the cloth may be prevented from slipping by working twice the number of motifs and having the cloth overhanging the back and the front equally or, if preferred, two heavy tassels may be attached to the back corners to weight the back. In either case, extra yarn must be provided for this purpose.

The arm rests are made by following crochet pattern 8, but four motifs are needed for the width and three motifs for the depth (twelve motifs). On a narrow chair arm the rests will stay in place, and indeed are enhanced, if a tassel is added to each corner. (For tassel instructions see page 45).

67   Detail of crochet motif used in patterns 8 and 9

10 Bedlinen edgings

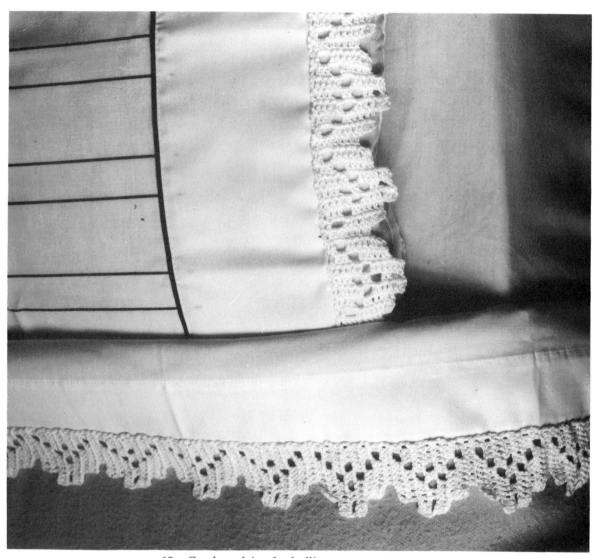

68 *Crochet edging for bedlinen, pattern 10*

The edging used in the photograph is neat, practical and easy to work; it has everything that is suited to a plain white or unfussy basic linen. It will wash and handle well and gives just a touch of interest to the linen.

This type of border has been chosen because it is worked widthways, forming a narrow strip in preference to working the foundation chain to the width of the sheet or pillowslip. The narrow strips can be tacked in place as you work to ensure a good fit.

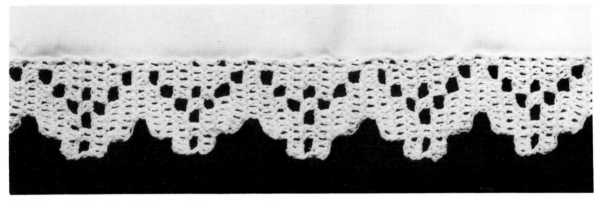

69   *Detail of crochet bedlinen edging, pattern 10*

Materials

2 balls (25 g) Twilley Lyscordet No 5 cotton to make sheet edging (see measurements)
1 ball to make one pillowslip edging
2 mm crochet hook

Measurements

5 cm (2 in) wide; sheet edging 182 cm (72 in) long; each pillowslip 102 cm (40 in) long.

Tension

A crochet hook should be used with this yarn to produce strips with a width of 5 cm (2 in).

To make

Make 11 ch.

1st row   1 tr in 4 th ch from hook, 1 tr in each ch to end, turn (*9 sts*).

2nd row   5 ch, 1 tr in 4th ch from hook, 1 tr in next ch, 1 tr in each of next 5 tr, 2 ch, miss 2 tr, 1 tr in next tr, 1 tr in top of turning ch, turn.

3rd row   3 ch (stands as first tr), miss 1 tr, 1 tr in next tr, 2 tr in 2-ch sp, 2 ch, miss 2 tr, 1 tr in each of 6 tr, turn.

4th row   5 ch, 1 tr in 4th ch from hook, 1 tr in next ch, 1 tr in each of next 4 tr, 2 ch, 2 tr in next 2-ch sp, 1 tr in each of next 3 tr, 1 tr in top of 3 ch, turn.

5th row   3 ch, miss 1st tr, 1 tr in each of next 3 tr, 2 ch, miss 2 tr, 2 tr in next 2-ch sp, 2 ch, miss 2 tr, 1 tr in each of next 2 tr, 2 ch, miss 2 tr, 1 tr in top of 3 ch, turn.

6th row   3 ch, miss 1 tr, 2 tr in 2-ch sp, 1 tr in each of next 2 tr, 2 tr in 2-ch sp, 2 ch, miss 2 tr, 2 tr in next 2-ch sp, 1 tr in each of next 3 tr, 1 tr in top of 3 ch, turn.

7th row   3 ch, miss 1 tr, 1 tr in each of next 3 tr, 2 ch, 2 tr in next 2-ch sp, 1 tr in each of next 4 tr, turn.

8th row   3 ch, miss 1 tr, 1 tr in each of next 5 tr, 2 tr in next 2-ch sp, 2 ch, miss 2 tr, 1 tr in next tr, 1 tr in top of 3 ch, turn.

9th row   3 ch, miss 1 tr, 1 tr in next tr, 2 tr in 2-ch sp, 1 tr in each of next 5 tr, turn.

The 2nd to 9th rows form the pattern. Repeat them until the strip fits, unstretched, along width of sheet or all round pillowslip opening.

To complete

Sew neatly to sheet edge or pillowslip opening. On pillowslip opening, join the first to last edges.

11   Alternative linen edgings

These edgings are as unobtrusive as the previous borders in their narrowness but offer a slightly more unusual quality.

Materials

These are similar to the linen edging requirements listed above in crochet pattern 10.

Measurements

The fan cluster pattern edging is 5 cm (2 in) wide.
The picot pattern edging is 3 cm (1¼ in) wide.
The length of the edging is optional.

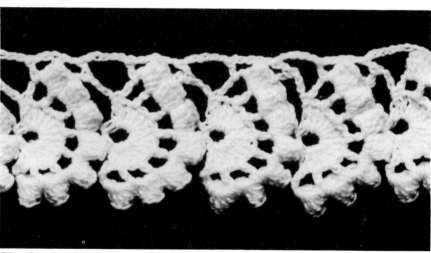

70   Crochet fan cluster linen edging, pattern 11

To make the fan cluster edging

Make 10 ch and join into ring with sl st.

1st row   3 ch, 14 tr into ring, 5 ch, turn.

2nd row   Miss first tr, (1 tr in next tr, 2 ch, miss 1 tr) 6 times, 1 tr in top of 3 ch, turn.

3rd row   *7 tr in next sp, remove hook from loop, insert hook into top of 3 ch then into the dropped loop and draw through all loops – cluster made – 3 ch; rep from * 5 times more, 1 cluster in last sp, 10 ch, turn.

4th row   Miss first 2 sps, (1 dc, 5 ch, 1 dc) all in next sp, 3 ch, turn.

5th row   13 tr in 5-ch loop, 1 dc in 10-ch loop, 5 ch, turn.

6th row   Miss first dc and first tr, (1 tr in next tr, 2 ch, miss 1 tr) 6 times, 1 tr in top of 3 ch, 3 ch, turn.

Rep 3rd to 6th rows for the pattern until the strip is the required length.

71   Crochet picot linen edging, pattern 11

To make the picot edging

Make 6 ch.

1st row   Into 6th ch from hook work 3 tr with 2 ch between, turn.

2nd row   Into centre tr work 3 tr with 2 ch between, 5 ch, turn.

The 2nd row forms the pattern. Rep the row until the strip is the required length. Do not turn at the end of the last row but work the heading across one long side thus:

*1 dc in next 5-ch loop, 5 ch; rep from * ending 3 ch, 1 tr in first st. Fasten off.

To make the picot edge: join the yarn to first 5-ch loop, 3 dc into loop, *4 ch, 1 dc in 4th ch from loop – picot made – 3 dc in same 5-ch loop, 2 ch, 3 dc in next 5-ch loop; rep from * ending with 3 dc, picot, 3 dc in last 5-ch loop. Fasten off.

To complete

Treat these edgings as the first border (pattern 10) and attach to the bedlinen in the same way.

12 Pram or cot cover

72   *Crochet pram or cot cover, pattern 12*

These small granny squares look attractive in cotton yarn for adult beds but are better suited to yarn that is soft to the touch for babies. A bonus for this type of cover is that, provided it has only lightweight wear, it is a simple matter to add more squares later to use it on the child's first grown-up size bed. Despite its delicate look the cover is worked with a thick hook and this, together with the fact that the squares are joined as you work, must make it one of the quickest gifts you could set out to make for a baby.

Materials
5 balls (50 g) Twilley Featherspun mohair-look
7 mm crochet hook

Measurements

71 cm (28 in) long; 61 cm (24 in) wide

Tension

Each square measures 10 cm (4 in) along each side edge.

To make each motif   Make 42 pieces.

Make 6 ch, join into ring with sl st.

1st round   8 dc into ring, join with sl st.

2nd round   3 ch, *leaving last loop on hook, work 2 tr in first st, yrh and draw through all loops, 3 ch, 3-tr cluster in next st, 1 ch; rep from * 3 times more, join with sl st to top of 3 ch.

3rd round   Sl st to ch sp, 3 ch (stands as 1st tr), 2 tr in same sp, 3 ch, 3 tr in same ch sp, *1 ch, miss next cluster, 1 tr in ch sp between next 2 clusters, 1 ch, 3 tr, 3 ch, 3 tr in next ch sp; rep from * 3 times, ending 1 ch, join with sl st to top of 3 ch.

4th round   With wrong sides of two motifs together, work 1 row dc along side edges to join. Fasten off.

When six squares have been joined in this way, fasten off and begin a new strip of squares.

To complete

Join the seven rows of six strips together with double crochet forming a ridge on the right side of the work as the squares are joined.

   For the border, join the yarn to one corner, 3 ch, 2 tr in same corner st, work 1 tr in each st all round outer edge, working 3 tr in each corner. Fasten off. Do not press.

73   Motif for crochet pram cover, pattern 12

13 Openwork round cushion cover

74 *Openwork crochet cover for round cushion, pattern 13*

Although this cover is worked in bold white yarn you will be able to link it into your colour scheme by using a blending colour for the lining fabric. The circular pattern may be repeated as a tablecloth to match, by omitting the popcorn stitches and continuing the rounds until the cloth is the desired size.

Materials
3 hanks (100 g) Twilley Handicraft No 1 Cotton
4 mm crochet hook

Measurement
Diameter of cushion cover is 46 cm (18 in).

Tension
Work to the equivalent of 18 trs to 10 cm (4 in) to produce the measurements given above.

To make

Make 5 ch, join into ring with sl st.

1st round   10 dc in ring, join with sl st.

2nd round   5 ch (stands as 1 tr, 2 ch), 1 tr in next dc, 2 ch, *1 tr in next dc, 2 ch; rep from * to end, join with sl st to 3rd of 5 ch (*10 tr*).

3rd round   Sl st into first sp, 3 ch (stands as 1 tr), 3 tr in same sp, *4 tr in next sp; rep from * to end, join with sl st to top of 3 ch.

4th round   5 ch, 1 tr in first tr, *miss 1 tr, (1tr, 1 ch, 1 tr) all in next tr; rep from * to end, join with sl st to 3rd of 5 ch.

5th round   Sl st into first sp, *5 ch, miss 2 tr, 1 dc in next ch sp; rep from * to end, ending with 5 ch, join to first sp.

6th round   Sl st to first sp, 3 ch, (1 tr, 2 ch, 2 tr) in same sp, *(2 tr, 2 ch, 2 tr) in each 5-ch sp; rep from * to end, join with sl st to top of 3 ch.

7th round   Sl st into first 2-ch sp, 3 ch, (1 tr, 2 ch, 2 tr) in same sp, *(2 tr, 2 ch, 2 tr) in each 2-ch sp; rep from * to end, join with sl st to top of 3 ch.

8th round   Sl st into first 2-ch sp, into this same sp work 5 tr, remove the hook from last tr, and insert in top of first tr, then through dropped loop, yrn and draw through all loops – popcorn made – 6 ch, *1 popcorn, 6 ch; rep from * to end, join with sl st to top of first popcorn.

9th round   Sl st into first 6-ch sp, 3 ch, (2 tr, 2 ch, 3 tr) in same 6-ch sp, (3 tr, 2 ch, 3 tr) in each 6-ch sp to end, join with sl st to top of 3 ch.

10th round   7 ch, *1 dc in next 2-ch sp, 5 ch, miss 3 tr, 1 tr in sp between trs, 5 ch; rep from * to end, join with sl st to 3rd of 7 ch.

11th round   Sl st into first sp, 3 ch, *(2 tr, 2 ch, 2 tr) in next 5-ch sp, (2 tr, 2 ch, 2 tr) in next 5-ch sp, 1 tr in next tr; rep from * to end, omitting last 1 tr, join with sl st to top of 3 ch.

12 round   Sl st into first sp, 3 ch, *(2 tr, 2 ch, 2 tr) in next 2-ch sp, (2 tr, 2 ch, 2 tr) in next 2-ch sp, 1 tr in next tr; rep from * to end, omitting last 1 tr, join with sl st to top of 3 ch.

13th round   As 12th round.

14th round   *(7 ch, 1 dc in 2-ch sp) twice, 7 ch, miss 2 tr, 1 dc in next tr; rep from * ending last rep, sl st to 1st of 7 ch instead of dc in next tr. Fasten off.

Work second piece in the same way.

To complete

Prepare cushion pad and lining. With wrong sides of crochet cover together, join yarn in a 7-ch loop, work this loop together with adjacent 7-ch loop of second side with 1 dc, *5 ch, join next two 7-ch loops with 1 dc; rep from * until approx one-third of the opening remains. Insert the cushion pad and continue joining the cover to end, ending 5 ch, join with sl st to 1st dc. Fasten off.

The cover should not need pressing but the last round may be improved by pressing to draw out these outer loops.

When removing the cushion for laundering the cover, make a note of how the two sides were joined so that they may be quickly rejoined again.

Conversion chart for knitting needles and crochet hooks

Knitting needles

UK		USA	Continental
Old sizes	Metric (mm)		(mm)
000	10	15	9
00	9	13	8·5
0	8	12	8
1	$7\frac{1}{2}$	11	7·5
2	7	$10\frac{1}{2}$	7
3	$6\frac{1}{2}$	10	6·5
4	6	9	6
5	$5\frac{1}{2}$	8	5·5
6	5	7	5
7	$4\frac{1}{2}$	6	4·5
8	4	5	4
9	$3\frac{3}{4}$	4	3·5
10	$3\frac{1}{4}$	3	–
11	3	2	3
12	$2\frac{3}{4}$	1	2·5
13	$2\frac{1}{4}$	0	–
14	2	00	2

Crochet hooks

UK (mm)	USA	Continental (mm)
7	$K/10\frac{1}{2}$	7
6·5	J/10	6·5
6	I/9	6
5·5	H/8	5·5
5	–	5
4·5	G/6	4·5
4	F/5	4
3·5	E/4	3·5
3	C/2	3
2·5	B/1	2·5
2	–	2

Glossary

Garter stitch: knit every row.

Knitwise: a term generally used in slipping stitches from the left-hand needle to the right by inserting the point of the right-hand needle into the loop, as if to knit it.

Purlwise: slipping a stitch from the left-hand needle to the right by inserting the point of the right-hand needle into the loop, as if to purl it.

Pass the slipped stitch over: the slipped stitch(es) is the first to be passed on to the right-hand needle; insert the point of the left-hand needle into this loop and lift it over the last stitch(es) on right-hand needle and off the needle.

Seed stitch: moss stitch, the method worked by reversing the k1 and p1 on consecutive rows.

Stocking stitch: stockinette, worked by one row knit, followed by one row purl.

Tension, gauge: the number of stitches and/or rows measured to a given number of centimetres or inches.

Through back of loop: knit or purl through the back of the stitch instead of the front; to knit, this means inserting the point of the right-hand needle into the centre of the loop from the right-hand side through to the back; to purl, this means inserting the point of the right-hand needle from the back from the left-hand side. The same technique is used for working two stitches together through back of loops.

*: this asterisk indicates the beginning of a pattern repeat; a semi-colon indicates the conclusion.

( ): brackets (parentheses) are used within pattern repeats where the method contained within the brackets is to be worked for the number of times indicated immediately following the bracket signs, e.g. (k2 tog) twice.

Yarn forward: a method of making a stitch by bringing the yarn forward between two knit stitches and over the top of the needle to work the following knit stitch.

Yarn round needle: this is the method of making a stitch when the yarn is already in the forward position and a purl stitch follows.

Crochet terms

UK	USA
double crochet	single crochet
half treble	half double crochet
treble	double crochet
double treble	treble
triple treble	double treble

Bibliography

Abbey, Barbara, *Knitting Lace*, The Viking Press Inc., New York, 1974
Stearns, Ann, *The Batsford Book of Crochet*, Batsford, 1981
Thomas, Mary, *Book of Knitting Patterns*, Hodder and Stoughton, 1935

Suppliers

To obtain information about stockists in the United Kingdom write to the following addresses:

For Twilley yarns (used throughout the book)
H. G. Twilley Ltd
Roman Mill
Stamford
Lincs
PE9 1BG

J. & P. Coats Ltd also specialise in cotton yarns but it is difficult to recommend exact alternatives. Readers are advised to work a tension sample before starting on any item.

J. & P. Coats Ltd
Domestic Marketing Division
Market Service Dept
39 Durham Street
Glasgow
G41 1BS

For Bond Knitting Systems
Bond Knitting Systems Ltd
79 High Street
Witney
Oxon
OX8 6LR

Index

Pages where illustrations appear are listed in *italic*.

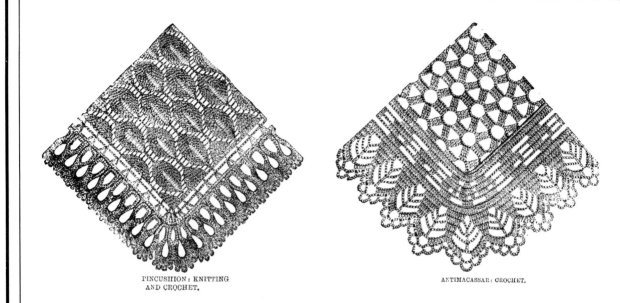

PINCUSHION: KNITTING
AND CROCHET.

ANTIMACASSAR: CROCHET.

KNITTED COUNTERPANE.

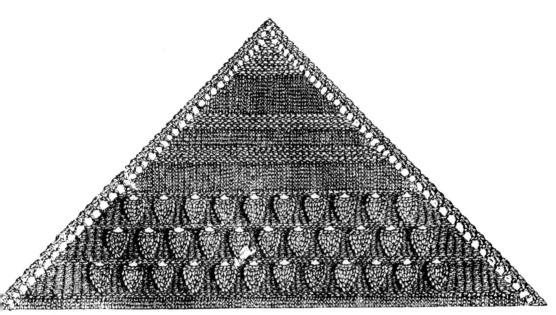

HALF OF KNITTED SQUARE FOR COUNTERPANE.

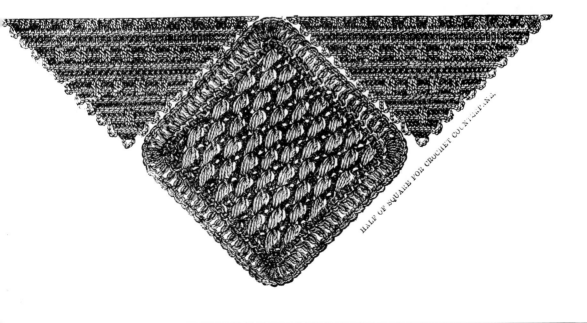

HALF OF SQUARE FOR CROCHET COUNTERPANE.